FSC
www.fsc.org
MIX
Papier aus verantwortungsvollen Quellen
Paper from responsible sources
FSC® C105338

Andreas Sossong

Institutional Asset Management

How are professional investors affected by legislature and corporate governance?

Anchor Academic
Publishing

Sossong, Andreas: Institutional Asset Management: How are professional investors affected by legislature and corporate governance?. Hamburg, Anchor Academic Publishing 2013

Buch-ISBN: 978-3-95489-088-0
PDF-eBook-ISBN: 978-3-95489-588-5
Druck/Herstellung: Anchor Academic Publishing, Hamburg, 2013

Bibliografische Information der Deutschen Nationalbibliothek:
Die Deutsche Nationalbibliothek verzeichnet diese Publikation in der Deutschen Nationalbibliografie; detaillierte bibliografische Daten sind im Internet über http://dnb.d-nb.de abrufbar.

Bibliographical Information of the German National Library:
The German National Library lists this publication in the German National Bibliography. Detailed bibliographic data can be found at: http://dnb.d-nb.de

Hermannstal 119k, 22119 Hamburg
http://www.diplomica-verlag.de, Hamburg 2013
Printed in Germany

ABSTRACT

This paper examines the current legislature and best practice corporate governance for institutional investors in Germany and the United States. Differences in investment regulation, compliance and disclosure requirements, as well as expense and tax schemes are identified for insurance companies and the pension fund industry. Based on current academic literature, hypotheses about the impact of different regulatory regimes are derived and tested empirically in a comparison between Germany and the United States over the last five years. Differences in asset allocation between the two countries are determined for both industries. It is shown that the strict quantitative regulation of asset allocation in Germany has no negative impact on institutional investors' performance, yet it reduces the realized risk measured through depreciation. A principal component regression reveals that asset allocation constitutes a relevant indicator for depreciation and performance in Germany. It can be inferred that the investment regulation in Germany poses little disadvantages for investors while it provides a significant risk reduction. This conclusion is confirmed by practitioners from the pension fund industry in Germany.

Table of Contents

List of Figures

List of Tables

List of Abbreviations

AnlV	Investment Ordinance
AuM	Assets under Management
BaFin	Federal Financial Supervisory Authority
BAKred	Federal Banking Supervisory Office
BAV	Federal Insurance Supervisory Office
BAWe	Federal Supervisory Office for the Securities Trading
Cap	Capitalization
Cf.	Confer
CRAN	Comprehensive R Archive Network
CTA	Contractual Trust Arrangement
DB	Defined Benefit
DC	Defined Contribution
DVVersoG	By-Law about the Execution of the Law for Public Pensions
EBRI	Employee Benefit Research Center
EC	European Commission
ERISA	Employee Retirement Income Security Act
Et sqq.	And the Following
ETF	Exchange Traded Fund
FinDAG	Financial Services and Integration Act
FY	Fiscal Year
GARP	Growth at a Reasonable Price
GCC	Cooperation Council for the Arab States of the Gulf
GDP	Gross Domestic Product
GER	Germany
HGB	German Code of Commercial Law
HML	Value Return Minus Growth Return
HPX	Housing Price Index Hedonic – Existing Home

IAIS	International Association of Insurance Supervisors
IAS	International Accounting Standard
IASB	International Accounting Standards Board
Ibid.	Ibidem
ICI	Investment Company Institute
ICP	Insurance Core Principals
IFRS	International Financial Reporting Standards
IGG	Investment Governance Group
IMA	Investment Management Association
IMF	International Monetary Fund
NAIC	National Association of Insurance Commissioners
OA	Other Assets
OECD	Organization for Economic Co-Operation and Development
p	Page
p.a.	per annum
Para.	Paragraph
PCR	Principal Component Regression
RechPensV	By-Law about the Financial Accounting of Insurance Companies
RechVersV	By-Law about the Financial Accounting of Pension Funds
REIT	Real Estate Investment Trust
S&P	Standard and Poor's Financial Services LLC
SEC	Securities and Exchange Commission
SMB	Small Capitalization Return Minus Large Capitalization Return
SRI	Socially Responsible Investment
Stdev	Standard Deviation
U.S. / US / USA	United States of America
UIT	Unit Investment Trust
UK	United Kingdom

USD	US-Dollar
VAG	Insurance Supervision Law
VaR	Value at Risk
VersAufsVO NWR	By-Law about Insurance Supervision in North Rhine-Westphalia
VW	Pension Fund for Professionals in Private Practice
WHU	Wissenschaftliche Hochschule für Unternehmensführung

List of Symbols

&	And
%	Percent
§	Paragraph
$	US-Dollar
€	Euro
R^2	Coefficient of Determination
w_A	Weight of Asset A in the Portfolio
σ_A	Volatility of Asset A
ρ_{AB}	Correlation of Assets A and B

1. Introduction

1.1 Problem Definition

> *Institutional investors in Germany have not seen this many opportunities to invest in stock markets for a long time – yet only very few take the courage to actually buy equities.*[1]
>
> *(Hans-Jürgen Möhring)*

With these words, Möhring summarizes a study conducted by Feri Eurorating Services among professional investors in Germany. The study shows that despite reasonable opportunities to earn money in financial markets, institutional investors are reluctant to take advantage of these. Obviously, other factors besides expected performance enter the equation that yields investment decisions of professional asset managers. This thesis tries to shed light on some of these factors, predominantly the legislative environment and corporate governance.

In the face of the aftermath of the recent financial crisis, the institutional asset management industry is confronted with several emerging challenges. Even as the falling asset prices have stabilized, managers are currently in stiffer market competition for investors' money,[2] which is not as available as it was before the crisis. On top of these challenges, the industry is facing the public's outcry for tighter regulation, followed by policy makers' decisions to chain financial markets.[3]

Institutional investors are confronted with various inherent external circumstances that are part of the decision-making process aiming at utility maximization. Such circumstances include investment regulations, compliance standards, level of market competition, tax systems as well as disclosure requirements. These factors can differ greatly between single countries around the world or even between regions within one country.

At the same time, most institutional investors are also faced with internal restrictions for their actions. Especially in highly industrialized countries, such as the United States or Germany, corporate governance of the investment organization often times limits the leeway for asset managers.

---

[1] Cf. Möhring (2010)
[2] Cf. Lannoo and Levin (2003), p2
[3] Cf. Tartler (2009)

When combining both external and internal constraints of the scope of action that an institutional investor encounters, clear differences in subsequent investment behavior between single investment firms and especially on an aggregated level between countries can be observed. The arising question is whether differences in investment performance between these investment styles can be measured and how exactly they can be explained.

1.2 Objective and Scope of the Paper

In the landscape of this status quo, the meaning of both internal and external restrictions for institutional investors' behavior forms the focus of the following scientific examination. This paper aims at identifying the key reasons for differences in investment behavior and the adjacent performance in theory. Subsequently, the study tests the emerging hypotheses empirically in order to find the valid influences that can explain investment, risk and performance discrepancies of institutional asset management between Germany and the United States.

After a presentation of the principles of institutional asset management, the latter are put into an international perspective where both external and internal environments for decision-making are examined. Conclusions on the expected impact on investment behavior are drawn before these hypotheses are tested empirically. Finally, implications for regulators and asset managers as well as research gaps are presented.

Among others, the following important questions are to be answered in this paper:

- What is the scientific approach behind institutional asset management?
- How can investment funds be classified and what are major recent developments in the industry?
- What are differences in the legal environment for institutional investors in Germany and the US?
- How is internal decision-making influenced by corporate governance?
- What expectations towards investment behavior derive from such differences and how do practitioners perceive the regulatory environment?
- Does the expected behavior take place in reality and can it be empirically confirmed?
- What conclusions can be drawn from the analysis and what are the implications for theory and practice of institutional asset management?

For complexity reasons, this paper is limited to differences in investment behavior between Germany and the United States. The thesis aims at identifying factors that influence the asset allocation and the investment performance of funds in comparison to their risk taken, opposed to an overall satisfaction of investors or other measures of quality, such as service quality. The data analysis is limited to institutional investors on the sponsoring level, i.e. insurances and pension funds. Other fund types, such as exchange traded funds or sovereign wealth funds are not part of this analysis. Not all hypotheses derived from differences in regulation and governance between the US and Germany can be tested explicitly in this thesis. While indications on the validity of some of these hypotheses can be seen in the data, others remain to be tested in future research.

1.3 Methodological Approach

1.3.1 Scientific Classification of Subject Area

Asset management plays a vital role in the system of financial intermediation[4] where it interacts with both private clients (retail management) and institutional clients (wholesale management)[5]. It is part of the banking sector and is thus to be included to the field of finance in an academic context. Lately, there has been a trend in research to extend the banking sector by the field of financial services to which investment activities can be attributed.[6]

Asset management further touches on other subcategories of finance that have recently evolved. Among others, one rapidly growing subcategory is Islamic finance, which increasingly gains importance as the client base and the investment focus of institutional investors have been shifting towards countries and investors that require conformity with Sharia (or Islamic law).[7] Another category that asset management is connected to is the field of taxation, which itself is a part of accounting. Both accounting and finance are sub-disciplines of business studies, a practice-oriented empirical science.

1.3.2 Methodology of the Analysis

Two methodological approaches are used in this paper. A theoretical part determines the principles of institutional asset management and the international perspective on the topic deductively, based on primary and secondary literature. Interviews with practitioners and regulators are conducted in order to gain further insights on how theory and practice are linked and to validate the hypotheses drawn.

---

[4] Cf. Walter (1998), p10
[5] Cf. Davis (2002a), p2
[6] Cf. Tilmes (2002), p9
[7] Cf. Gait and Worthington (2007), p1 et sqq.

The practical part of this thesis aims at validating the derived suppositions of how investment behavior is affected by different external and internal circumstances in different countries. This is done through examination of primary and secondary empirical data on a scientific basis.[8] The conducted analyses make use of descriptive statistics, principal component analysis, principal component regression and hypothesis testing.

1.4 Composition of the Paper

Figure 1 depicts the composition of this paper that is structured into three main parts – theory, practice and conclusion.

Figure 1: Thematic Composition of the Paper with Reference to the Respective Chapters

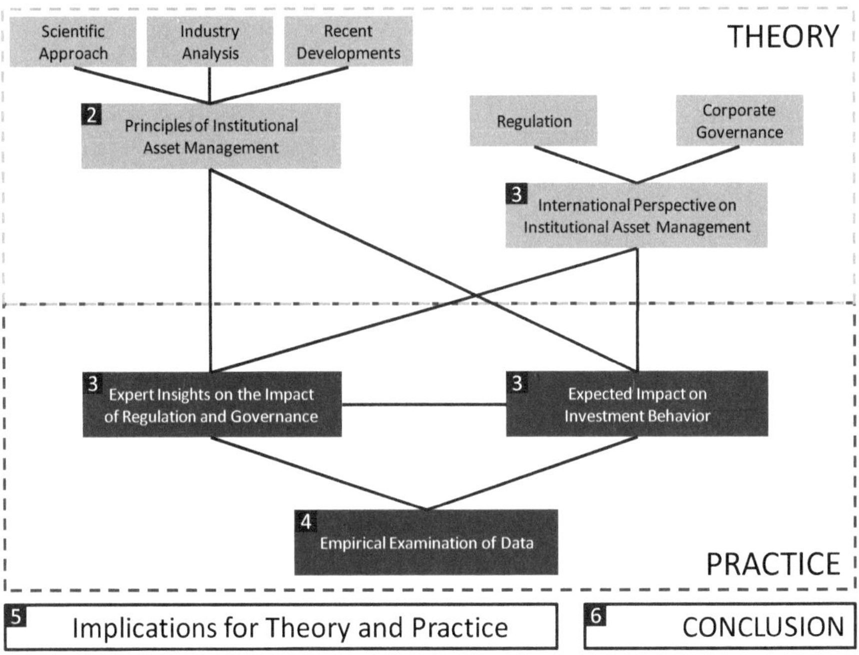

Source: Own illustration

[8] Primary data from company reports and news services as well as secondary data from the EBRI is used

The theoretical part of this thesis is built on two major themes, asset management as well as regulation and corporate governance. Chapter 2 deals with the principals of institutional asset management and provides a basis for further elaboration on the topic. Its three core parts are the scientific approach of asset management, a comprehensive industry analysis and a look at recent developments in the field. The scientific approach compares investment styles of funds, elaborates on asset allocation and provides explanations for the significance of the industry. The industry analysis provides a classification of investment funds and explains major differences amongst them. Recent developments in the field include a recap of the financial crisis and a description of current trends in the industry.

Chapter 3 puts the institutional asset management industry into an international perspective. It deals with differences in the legal environment of funds between countries and corporate governance. The legal environment includes comparisons and analyses that institutional investors from the US and Germany face concerning market regulations, compliance rules, disclosure restrictions, expenses and taxes. Internal decision-making processes for both countries are highlighted on the base of corporate governance best practices for the insurance industry and pension funds.

Chapter 3 also bridges the gap between theory and practice by including two of the three main blocks of the practical part of this thesis. Experts' perspectives on the impact of investment regulation and corporate governance are voiced by both a regulator and asset managers. The subchapter on the expected impact on investment behavior draws conclusions to the theoretical circumstances described previously and provides hypotheses that are to be tested in the third, practice-oriented part of this paper, the empirical examination of the data. This analysis is conducted in chapter 4.

Chapter 5 and 6 conclude the thesis and recap the findings. In addition, they provide implications for theory and practice and show future research opportunities in the associated scientific environment.

1.5 Definitions

The core terms of this work are investment behavior, institutional investors and asset management. Before a deeper dive into the topic in chapter 2, the terms are defined and separated from neighboring topics.

1.5.1 Asset Management and Institutional Investors

The terms asset management and investment management are used interchangeably in this paper. Asset management is generally used in the context of pooled investing, whose origins date back to the late 18th century.[9] The original idea of investment pooling was to provide a means of diversification for private investors with common financial goals.[10] While diversification is still one of the key elements of asset management, the range of investors is now broader than ever, including individuals, companies and trusts.

According to the National Association of U.S. Investment Companies[11], registered investment companies in the United States can currently be classified as one of four of the following types: open-end mutual funds, closed-end funds, exchange traded funds (ETFs) and unit investment trusts (UITs). In addition to retail or wholesale-oriented companies such as banks, insurances or independent fund management firms, the term asset management also refers to organizations whose sole purpose is to invest its assets.[12] All of these organizations are summarized as institutional investors. Further examples of such investors include pension funds, hedge funds and sovereign wealth funds. Insurance companies, pension plans and pension funds for professionals in private practice play an outstanding role in this paper as they form the foundation of the international comparison and empirical study.

1.5.2 Investment Behavior

Investment behavior in this thesis is defined as the specific asset allocation chosen by an institutional investor in conjunction with the applied risk management and the resulting investment performance. Investment behavior is thus closely related to investment styles, a more frequently used term in finance. Ever since Sharpe[13] as well as Fama and French[14] introduced the notion of investment or equity style to practitioners and academics in the early 1990s, the idea has been widely accepted in the investment community.[15] This is due to the fact that numerous researchers, e.g. Grinold[16], Davis[17], He and Ng[18] or Fama and French[19] have confirmed the original result that investment styles have larger explanatory power for

---

[9] Cf. Rouwenhorst (2004), p5 et sqq.
[10] Cf. ICI (2010), p218
[11] Cf. ICI (2010), p187
[12] Cf. Davis (2002a), p2
[13] Cf. Sharpe (1992), p7 et sqq.
[14] Cf. Fama and French (1992), p427 et sqq.
[15] Cf. Hwang and Satchell (2007), p598
[16] Cf. Grinold (1993), p28 et sqq.
[17] Cf. Davis (1994), p1579 et sqq.
[18] Cf. He and Ng (1994), p599 et sqq.
[19] Cf. Fama and French (e.g. 1993, 1996)

cross-sectional variation in equity returns than the beta factor.[20] According to Keim and Madhavan[21], the investment style of an investor is also one of the two determining factors for investment performance. Coggin, Fabozzi and Rahman[22] validate the segregation by Haughton and Christopherson into four basic investment styles that are largely based on asset allocation[23]: Earnings growth, market-oriented, price-driven and small capitalization. These four investment styles have set the foundation for future research in the field and thus a more detailed description is provided in chapter 2.1.1.

2. Principles of Institutional Asset Management

After defining the key terms of this paper, the following chapter provides a detailed description of the principles of institutional asset management. Based on this depiction, the regulation and governance of the institutional asset management industry will be put in an international perspective and compared across countries.

2.1 Scientific Approach

A definition of the term asset management has been provided in section 1.5.1 of this thesis. In order to be able to understand the value proposition of asset management funds and compare their behavior in the light of different external environments and internal guidelines, it is important to take a look at different investment styles first.

2.1.1 Investment Styles

Barberis and Shleifer identify two major reasons why both institutional as well as private investors might pursue style investing. First, categorization of funds into investment styles reduces the problem of choice and allows a more efficient processing of information. Second, benchmarking is made easier and the performance of asset managers is more observable since the classification inevitably creates a peer group of funds.[24]

A brief definition of investment styles has been given in chapter 1.5.2 of this paper. A closer look at these so-called Frank Russell style portfolios is now taken following Haughton and Christopherson[25]:

---

[20] Cf. Faff (1999), p3
[21] Cf. Keim and Madhavan (1997), p265
[22] Cf. Coggin, Fabozzi and Rahman (1993), p1043
[23] Cf. Haughton and Christopherson (1989)
[24] Cf. Barberis and Shleifer (2003), p162
[25] Cf. Haughton and Christopherson (1989)

- *Earnings Growth:* This strategy focuses mainly on earnings and revenue growth of investment targets and tries to identify above-average growth prospects. These prospects can stem from a historic trend as well as other circumstances including momentum based on company, industry and economic factors.
- *Market-Oriented:* The market-oriented strategy aims at representing either the whole spectrum of the financial market or sub-sectors, such as certain industries. Thus, in general, market-oriented funds are highly diversified.
- *Price-Driven:* Also known as value investing, this strategy focuses on the low price proportion of the market, i.e. securities with low valuations relative to the broad market.
- *Small Capitalization:* As the name already suggests, this strategy covers companies with a small market capitalization. They may be unseasoned and rapidly growing, or sometimes simply small businesses with a long history. Characteristics include below-market dividend yields, above-market betas and high residual risk compared to the broad market.

Many investment managers work along two of these categories, namely the market size of their fund and the classification as value or growth. For the latter, academic research (e.g. Fama and French[26] or Chan, Karceski and Lakonishok[27]) identified the book-to-market ratio of a firm as the most important ratio. In their analysis, Chan, Chen and Lakonishok[28] include past stock performance and find that it is closely related to the investment strategy based on book-to-market ratios.

Fama and French[29] developed a three-factor model with which funds can be classified concerning their investment style. This is done by estimating the following regression:

$$R_{it} - R_{ft} = a_i + b_i\left(R_{mt} - R_{ft}\right) + s_i SMB_t + h_i HML_t + e_{it}$$

where R_{it} equals the return of fund i for month t, R_{ft} the risk-free return for month t and R_{mt} the market return of month t. SMB_t is the realization on the capitalization factor for month t and HML_t is the realization of the value factor for month t. The factor loading s_i on SMB tends to be positive for small stocks and negative for large stocks. Similarly, a positive factor loading h_i indicates sensitivity to the value factor of stocks, whereas a negative loading indicates a growth tilt. Thus, it is possible to categorize funds as small or large cap-oriented as

---

26 Cf. Fama and French (e.g. 1992 and 1993)
27 Cf. Chan, Karceski and Lakonishok (1998), p159 et sqq.
28 Cf. Chan, Chen and Lakonishok (2002), p1428
29 Cf. Fama and French (1993)

well as value or growth-driven based on their SMB and HML slopes respectively. a_i is the regression's intercept and e_{it} refers to the error term.

While much research effort has been spent on determining whether certain style characteristics dominate others and whether the classification into the size and value-growth dimensions is empirically valid, only little attention has been drawn to the effect of style consistency of a fund. Brown and Harlow started to fill this gap and come to the conclusion that indeed style consistency, i.e. a low tracking error towards the benchmark and/or model-based style consistency, leads to lower portfolio turnover in the fund, a positive relationship to future actual and relative returns as well as a higher persistence of fund performance over time.[30]

These results emphasize the importance of investment styles in asset management.Figure 2 depicts an example of the application of the two-dimension investment style in practice.

Figure 2: Example of Investment Style Application in Practice

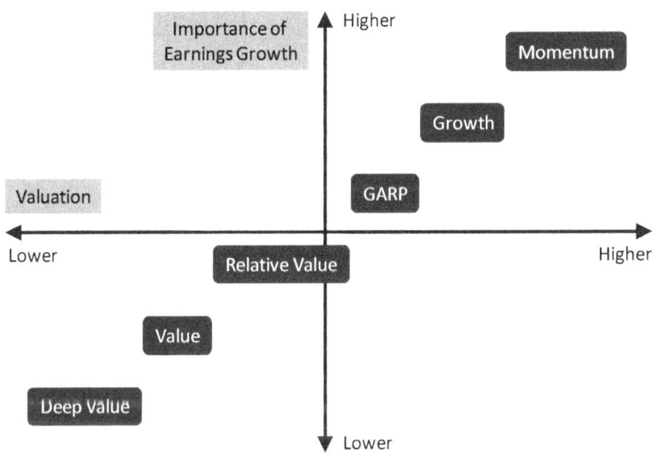

Source: Own illustration after Sionna Investment Managers[31]

The Fama and French three-factor model and the underlying benchmark factors have been affirmed many times by other researchers and are widely accepted in the academic research community. However, their model has so far exclusively been used for equity-only portfolios. An application to a multi-asset portfolio appears possible, yet the model would be overly specified for the purpose of this study.

---

[30] Cf. Brown and Van Harlow (2002)
[31] Cf. Sionna Investment Managers (2010)

2.1.2 Asset Allocation

Having introduced the predominant investment styles in both practice and academic research, the topic of asset allocation builds the core of this chapter. Knowledge on asset allocation is essential to understand the differences in investment behavior of funds that shape the asset management industry in all parts of the world.

Sharpe defines asset allocation as the allocation of an investor's portfolio among a number of major asset classes. These major asset classes include bills, intermediate-term government bonds, long-term government bonds, corporate bonds, mortgage-related securities, large-capitalization value stocks, large- capitalization growth stocks, medium- capitalization stocks, small- capitalization stocks, non-US bonds, European stocks and Japanese stocks.[32] This list is not absolute; nevertheless, it presents a good overview of the range of asset classes generally used in academic research.

The mean-variance analysis of Markowitz[33] has provided a strong foundation for asset allocation by emphasizing the ability to reduce financial risk through diversification. However, several critically important factors are left out in Markowitz' analysis, including the dynamics of financial markets. Since Samuelson[34] as well as Merton[35] introduced their multi-period portfolio optimization models, it has been understood that the solution for optimal long-term investing can be a different one compared to the optimal solution of the static mean-variance analysis. The common denominator of these models is that the addition of an asset to a portfolio decreases the unsystematic risk of the portfolio, as long as there is no perfect correlation between the new asset and one already existing in the portfolio. Also, the risk in these models is always measured in terms of variance. However, this leaves a gap for investors who want to optimize their portfolio and whose risk is composed of other factors than variance, e.g. asymmetric risk measures. Harlow addresses this issue and introduces portfolio optimization with a downside risk approach; yet he affirms the intuition of risk reduction through the addition of non-perfectly correlated assets.[36] In this context, asset allocation is of crucial importance to investors since in general, the correlation among different asset classes is lower than that of assets within one asset class. Therefore, optimizing a portfolio can generally be done with little complication through the use of various asset

---

32 Cf. Sharpe (1992), p11
33 Cf. Markowitz (1952)
34 Cf. Samuelson (1969)
35 Cf. Merton (1969)
36 Cf. Harlow (1991)

classes. In doing so, two types of asset allocation have to be distinguished: strategic asset allocation and tactical asset allocation.

The strategic asset allocation, a term coined by Brennan, Schwartz and Lagnado,[37] describes the far-sighted response to time-varying investment opportunities. Thus, it can be seen as the fundamental policy mix that a portfolio follows. Tactical asset allocation, in turn, refers to adjustments of a portfolio's asset allocation in the nearer term. This can be done either systematically or with discretion. The latter is based on the asset manager's judgment of the near-future market development, whereas the former uses quantitative investment models to systematically exploit inefficiencies or temporary imbalances to the equilibrium state among different asset classes.[38]

The popular opinion among asset managers is that there is no optimal asset allocation among cash, stocks and bonds, which is inconsistent with the mutual-fund separation theorem. The latter states that all investors should hold the same composition of risky assets.[39] So far, no satisfactory explanation has been found for this inconsistency between practitioners and academic research.

An interesting discovery in the light of the topic of this paper has been made by Ang and Bekaert.[40] Ang and Bekaert found that correlations between international equity markets tend to increase in times of highly volatile bear markets, which leaves doubt about the importance of asset allocation, especially in the international context. The conclusion of their paper is that, even with such correlation changes in regime shifts, international diversification is a valuable part of asset allocation. Furthermore, the costs of ignoring the different regimes increase when a conditionally risk-free asset can be held.

2.1.3 Sustainable Outperformance of Benchmarks

One major reason for the existence of the double to triple-digit trillion Dollar industry of asset management is the belief of capital sponsors, that asset managers can consistently outperform financial markets and their respective benchmarks. Brown and Goetzmann[41] analyze fund performance while accounting for a survivorship bias and find that relative performance persistence exists. However, it turns out that the outperforming funds have a high correlation among each other which suggests the possibility that they are loading up on a macroeconomic

37 Cf. Brennan, Schwartz and Lagnado (1997)
38 Cf. Stockton and Shtekhman (2010), p1
39 Cf. Canner, Mankiw and Weil (1997), p181 et sqq.
40 Cf. Ang and Bekaert (2002)
41 Cf. Brown and Goetzmann (1995)

factor unassociated with the major components of equity returns. Using Fama-French factors, Carhart[42] provides evidence for short-term persistence in equity fund returns. He discovers that the reasons for the top decile funds' outperformance are due to the momentum of stocks, differences in expense ratios and differences in transaction costs. However, the discovered outperformance of 8 percent of the top decile versus the bottom decile is mostly accountable to the extreme underperformance of bad funds. Elton, Gruber and Blake[43] blame the bad performance of the lowest decile on the very high expenses of these funds. They conclude that funds that did well in the past tend to do well in the future, also on a risk-adjusted basis. They further discover that using modern portfolio theory to form optimal portfolios based on past information leads to the selection of mutual funds with a positive return compared to a portfolio of funds with equal amounts invested in the funds considered. This outperformance is both economically and statistically significant. Finally, Grinblatt and Titman[44] also confirm that there is positive persistence in mutual fund performance. In addition, they find persistence differences in fees and transaction costs across funds, yet state that this is not the only explanation for performance differences. In their opinion, the past performance of an asset manager provides useful information for capital sponsors concerning their choice of funds in the portfolio.

The evidence of the sponsors' belief about outperformance of benchmarks through professional asset managers can be described as mixed. However, certain patterns can be observed when creating rankings of fund managers. Some managers consistently appear near the bottom of such rankings and it is the goal of the sponsor to reduce the likelihood of realizing abnormal returns by selecting these managers.[45]

An interesting addition to the mentioned research is provided by Davis,[46] who conducted an empirical analysis to identify a potential relationship between consistent outperformance of asset managers and their investment style. Using the Fama-French portfolios as benchmarks over a 33-year period, Davis concludes that no investment style generates positive abnormal returns. The performance persistence among the best-performing growth funds is not sustainable beyond one year. Among small cap managers, he discovers a persistence of poor performance in the United States. Similar results have been reached in a study conducted in the United Kingdom by Quigley and Sinquefield.[47] Davis further states that not even the value

---

[42] Cf. Carhart (1997)
[43] Cf. Elton, Gruber and Blake (1996)
[44] Cf. Grinblatt and Titman (1992)
[45] Cf. Davis (2000), p27
[46] Cf. Davis (2001)
[47] Cf. Quigley and Sinquefield (2000)

premium in common stock returns produced by the market in the analyzed period was captured by funds; even the extreme decile of the HML (value) factor funds ranking failed to do so.

Although the evidence of asset managers' outperformance towards the benchmark is not a clear one, Davis states that to a certain degree it depends on the style of the fund. So, there should be an implication for sponsor behavior concerning their choice of funds. The following chapter will provide an overview of the the industry makeup and also contains additional information about four important types of funds that are actively managed by asset managers.

2.2 Industry Examination and Classification of Funds

One way to categorize the asset management industry is according to the type of funds managed by the investment manager. Figure 3 depicts the most important types of funds, as well as their average global asset allocation. Real estate investment trusts (REITs) and exchange traded funds (ETFs) are beyond the scope of this thesis and will thus not be discussed explicitly.

Figure 3: Types of Funds and Their Average Global Asset Allocation

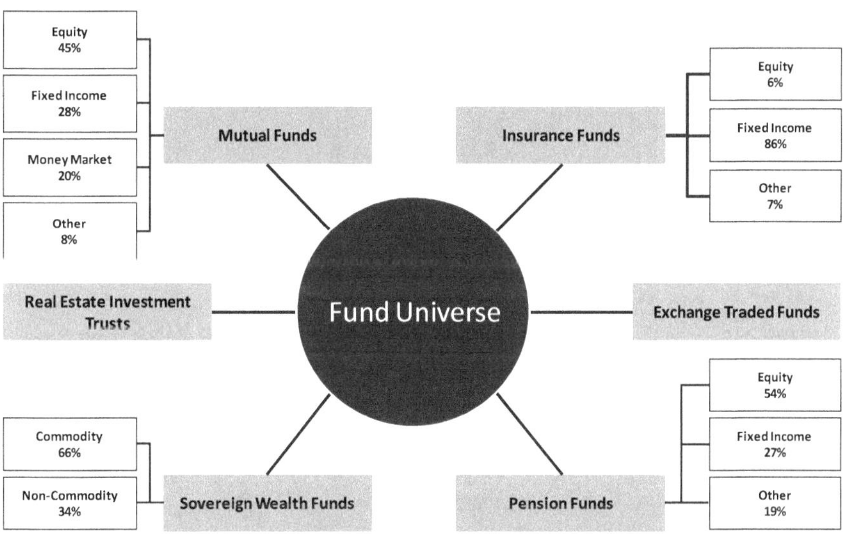

Source: Own illustration; data from ICI[48], IMA[49], Judd and Yin[50] and Maslakovic[51]

---

[48] Cf. ICI(2010), p23
[49] Cf. IMA (2010), p25
[50] Cf. Judd and Yin (2010), p5

Concerning asset allocation, the global investment management industry observed both a decline of money invested in the money market of 2.2 percent and an increase of 2.2 percent in equity investments. Fixed income assets increased by 1.4 percent while balanced hybrids, structured products and alternative investments all declined by around 0.5 percent each compared to the end of 2008.[52] The current asset allocation structure worldwide categorized by fund type according to the Fund Management 2010 Report by TheCityUK[53] is depicted in Figure 4.

The variable that measures the absolute size of the asset management industry is called assets under management. Since this variable highly depends on what the author of a survey considers a professional asset manager, the actual number is hard to assess. Estimates for the global industry range from 52.6 Trillion USD[54] to 105 Trillion USD[55].

Figure 4: Global Fund Allocation in Trillion USD by Type of Fund

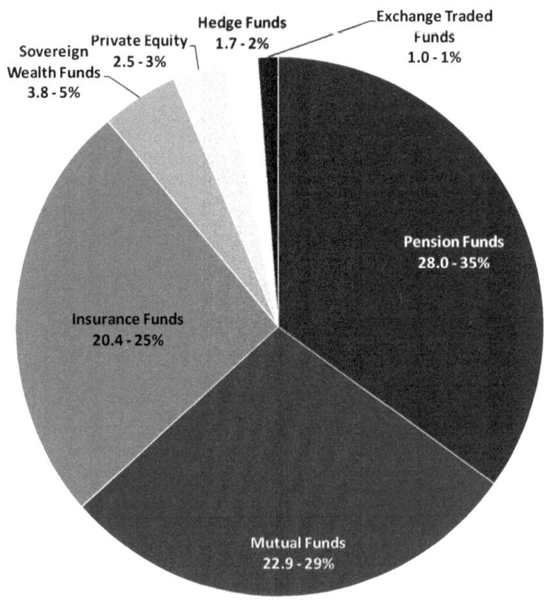

Source: Own illustration after Maslakovic (2010)[56]

51 Cf. Maslakovic (2010), p4 et sqq.
52 Cf. Kramer et al. (2010), p8
53 Cf. Maslakovic (2010), p1
54 Cf. Kramer et al. (2010), p4
55 Cf. Maslakovic (2010), p1
56 Cf. Ibid.

The industry has seen a strong rebound of assets under management globally following the financial crisis. As depicted in Figure 5, the recovery has taken place in all regions of the world, led by Asia ex Japan and Latin America. However, this astonishing development is based on the recovery of asset prices rather than an inflow of new sponsor money. In fact, only one percentage point was coming from fresh money according to the Global Asset Management Report 2010 by The Boston Consulting Group.[57] The recent developments of the industry are summarized in section 2.3 of this paper.

Figure 5: Development of Global Assets Under Management with p.a. Growth Rates

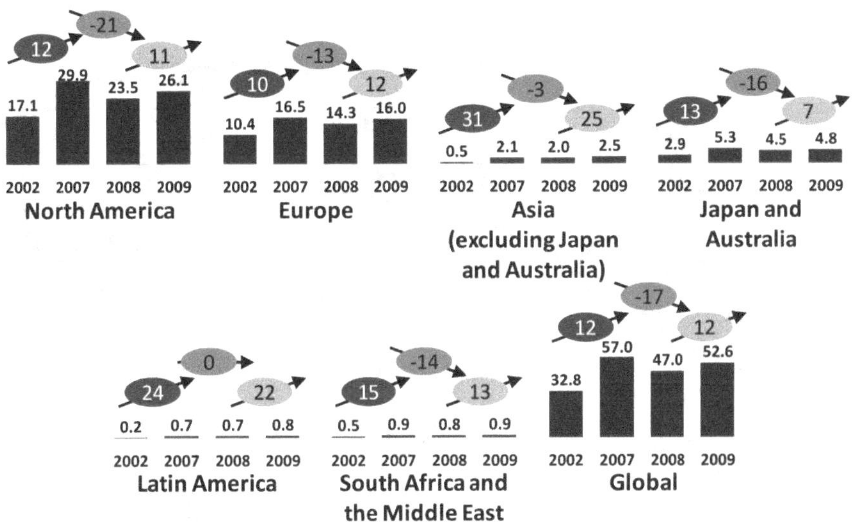

Source: Own illustration after Kramer et al. (2010)

Having provided a short overview of the classification of funds and the current state of the industry, the following four sections will dive deeper into the four most important types of funds and summarize the current academic literature in the field.

2.2.1 Pension Funds

Pension funds are generally established by a company to provide retirement income for its employees. They pose the largest type of fund, ahead of mutual funds and insurance funds, and can be important shareholders for both private and public companies. Besides the fund management through a sponsoring company, there are various different types of pension fund schemes used worldwide. In Germany, a system of pension funds for professionals in private practice, such as lawyers or doctors, constitutes a form of private financial precaution. Corporate pension funds also do not have to be defined as such, but can choose to operate as a

[57] Cf. Kramer et al. (2010), p7

Contractual Trust Arrangement (CTA) instead, which is accompanied by advantages like additional insolvency security, improved credit ratings for the parent company and less regulation through the insurance supervision, also towards investments. In the United States, most pension money is managed on a private basis, even though companies are often times involved in providing funding through the 401(k) plan.

According to Vittas[58], pension funds are not only a source of long-term savings to support the development of bond and equity markets, but can also be a positive force for innovation, corporate governance and privatization, assuming the interplay between pension funds and financial markets is set in the right frame by policymakers. The advantages of a functioning pension fund system can be especially beneficial to emerging countries. Here, pension funds can act as catalysts for the development of efficient trading and settlement systems, the adoption of modern accounting and auditing standards as well as the promotion of meaningful information disclosure.

As pension funds can be major shareholders of a listed company, many of them have pursued an active role in corporate decision-making. Del Guercio and Hawkins[59] took on the subject of pension fund activism and discover that for the most activist funds, shareholder proposals are often followed by significant additional corporate governance activity and broad corporate change, such as a restructuring or sale of assets. While they conclude that the shareholder proposals are effective in promoting change at the target companies and that pension fund activism is not inconsistent with fund value maximization, there is no evidence that this activism has a significant impact on stock returns or key accounting measures.

One common phenomenon observed in the pension fund industry is called window dressing. Window dressing occurs towards the end of a quarter, especially towards the end of the fourth quarter of a year. At the end of a quarter, fund reports including the current holdings of shares are published and "nobody wants to be caught showing last quarter's disasters. [...] You throw out the duds because you don't want to have to apologize for and defend a stock's presence to clients even though your investment judgment may be to hold.", as a fund manager is quoted by Jansson.[60] The easiest and most common way to execute window dressing is the sale of loser shares that have crashed during the preceding quarter. Pension funds can also reduce the pace of sale of winners, increase the purchase of winners and reduce

---

[58] Cf. Vittas (1996)
[59] Cf. Del Guercio and Hawkins (1999)
[60] Cf. Jansson (1983), p139

the purchases of losers to impress the sponsors with the current constitution of the portfolio.[61] Lakonishok et al. confirm that the phenomenon of window dressing is certainly an issue in the pension fund industry, especially among small funds.[62]

Unlike the performance of mutual funds, pension funds' performance has not been vastly analyzed. Coggin, Fabozzi and Rahman[63] are among the few academic researchers that entered into the area of pension funds performance. They discover that, regardless of the choice of the benchmark portfolio or estimation model, the selectivity measure is positive on average, whereas the timing measure is negative. When managers are classified by the Fama and French investment styles, both selectivity and timing appear to be more sensitive to the choice of the benchmark. Coggin, Fabozzi and Rahman however cannot explain why some active fund managers are able to provide substantial risk-adjusted outperformance while most of them fail to do so. Blake, Lehmann and Timmermann[64] discuss that market timing and the asset selection of a pension fund tend to be far less important for a pension fund's performance than the strategic asset allocation discussed in section 2.1.2 of this thesis. They discover that the weights of different assets in their studied funds have a slow mean-reversing tendency to a common strategic asset allocation, which in turn can explain most of the time-series variation of portfolio returns.

Also focusing on pension fund performance in his paper, Davis[65] examines the potential and actual role that international investments play in the pension fund industry. He shows that despite caveats and restrictions on international investments for pension funds, they would allow the funds to achieve superior performance in terms of risk and return. In fact, additional government regulation is undesirable and even unnecessary since there is a natural home bias for investments by pension funds.

2.2.2 Mutual Funds

The mutual fund structure is a very common one for a fund that collects and pools money from investors and typically invests the sponsors' money in securities such as equities, bonds, the money market, commodities etc. Even though this study is not focused on the mutual fund industry, it is pivotal to provide a substantiated state of knowledge in this field, as mutual

---

61 Cf. Haugen and Lakonishok (1988)
62 Cf. Lakonishok et al. (1991)
63 Cf. Coggin, Fabozzi and Rahman (1993)
64 Cf. Blake, Lehmann and Timmermann (1999)
65 Cf. Davis (2002b)

funds mark an important investment vehicle for institutional investors, e.g. German insurance companies invested around 25 percent of their capital assets into mutual funds in 2009.[66]

Mutual funds play an important role in the retail part of asset management. For retail investors, performance is a crucial decision criterion for a fund. Thus, as mentioned in section 2.1.3 of this thesis, researchers have analyzed the performance of funds thoroughly. Sharpe as well as Treynor laid the base for analyzing the performance of mutual funds in the mid 1960s. Both Sharpe[67] and Treynor[68] are pioneers that revolutionized the way mutual funds' performance is examined today by including simple risk measures and putting the absolute performance of funds into perspective to the risk taken to achieve this return. The Treynor ratio (T) relates the outperformance of the fund versus the risk free rate to the portfolio's beta:

$$T_i = \frac{r_i - r_f}{\beta_i}$$

where r_i is the return of portfolio i, r_f is the risk free return and β_i is the beta of portfolio i. The Sharpe ratio (S) is very similar to the Treynor ratio, but uses portfolio volatility instead of beta as the relevant risk measure:

$$S_i = \frac{r_i - r_f}{\sigma_i}$$

Both the Treynor and the Sharpe ratio are still used widely in the industry today.

The topic of investment styles mentioned in chapter 2.1.1 of this thesis is another important topic when differentiating mutual funds. Even though Fama and French and the following researchers have largely determined the most important investment styles for mutual funds, doubt remains about the granularity and the informative value of this classification. Brown and Goetzmann[69] find that the existing classifications do a poor job at forecasting differences in future performance. Avoiding the pitfalls and limitations of the statistical estimations used to analyze the traditional classifications, Brown and Goetzmann show that their applied switching regression technology dominates other style classifications and does a better job than classifying funds according to observed factor loadings.

Aside from looking at mutual fund performance, it is interesting to analyze other factors that impact capital flows between mutual funds, such as the cost of search. Sirri and Tufano[70] studied the flow of money into and out of mutual funds in order to better understand the

---

66 Cf. BaFin (2010b), p88
67 Cf. Treynor (1965)
68 Cf. Sharpe (1966)
69 Cf. Brown and Goetzmann (1997)
70 Cf. Sirri and Tufano (1998)

behavior of the retail market on both the buy and sell side. They find that investors behave irrationally in the sense that they invest too heavily into well-performing funds and at the same time miss to divest from badly performing funds at a similar rate. In addition, investors' behavior towards fees appears to be highly irrational, which is also reflected in capital flows. A third point mentioned by Sirri and Tufano states that investors respond to risk in their portfolios, which may offset mutual fund managers' incentive to increase fund volatility. In contrast to Gruber[71], who claims that investors' behavior to invest in mutual funds with net inflows and divest from those with net outflows is rational since this strategy beats passive index funds, Sirri and Tufano separate a fund's marketing effort as a key driver for net inflows. Funds with large marketing expenditure enjoy a much stronger performance-flow relationship than competing funds.

2.2.3 Insurance Funds

Insurances are a form of hedging for risk, mostly in form of an uncertain loss. For capital investments, life insurances are especially interesting due to their longevity, the subsequent need for adequate long-term capital management as well as liability issues they face. A life insurance thus serves two purposes, the cover against risk of death or survivance and the investment service involving guarantees of future capital security and long-term yield.[72]

Wehrle[73] adjusts the portfolio theory by Markowitz and Tobin to examine the actual portfolios of life insurance companies. The theory is modified appropriately to account for the particular investment risks associated with the liabilities of life insurance companies. He identifies three different types of life insurance investments:

- *The Capital Security Portfolio:* Setting the investor and manager in a principal-agency framework, Penman determines the three most important traditional objectives of the trustee investment as safety, yield and liquidity.[74] This type of life insurance investment caters to exactly this ranking of investor needs by prioritizing risk minimization to yield and taking appropriate investments.
- *The Income Security Portfolio:* While the first portfolio type is defensive towards default risk, this second type is defensive towards income risk. The emphasis of the life insurance's guarantee of a long-term yield lies on the long-term solvency position of

71 Cf. Gruber (1996)
72 Cf. Kirton and Haynes (1953)
73 Cf. Wehrle (1961), p70 et sqq.
74 Cf. Penman (1933)

the company. The general aim of the portfolio manager in this case is "keeping long", suggesting the purchase of long maturities.

- *The Competitive or Yield Portfolio:* The competitive portfolio type affirms the advantages of increased yields while not denying the importance of default and income risk. Wehrle suggests sizeable liquidity holdings as a transactions balance to facilitate opportune purchases.

Adams [75] examines the suggestion that contracting incentives for managers to increase investment earnings are dependent upon organizational factors, such as ownership structure and firm size. He indicates that return on invested assets is positively associated with stock companies; large and highly levered companies and entities engaged in riskier activities. Life insurance companies holding relatively more financial to nonfinancial assets have a low investment yield, contrary to theoretical predictions.

More recently, the issue of pricing of various insurance products has been the major focus of research in this field, for example Frantz, Chenut and Walhin,[76] who compare the Black-Scholes method to the actuarial approach for policy pricing.

2.2.4 Sovereign Wealth Funds

The following section is devoted to a rather new type of fund in the financial market. Even though sovereign wealth funds have existed since the 1950s, they have dramatically gained importance over the last 10-15 years. Yet, the absolute market size of sovereign wealth funds is of no comparison to mutual, pension or insurance funds, as depicted in Figure 4. Due to their uniqueness and projected importance in the future, they are a highly interesting investment vehicle to look at.

Sovereign wealth funds are state-owned investment funds that invest into a broad range of assets. Due to their relatively small investment restrictions, sovereign wealth funds show a greater diversity in their asset allocation than other types of funds. Since many times these funds are held by the central bank of the respective country, investments in foreign exchange are common. The tendency to have large proportions of the money invested in commodities can be derived from the origin of many of these funds in the Middle East, as well as the investment into gold by the central banks. Sovereign wealth funds are based on current account surpluses and will become less important only if the countries with large surpluses begin to run prolonged current account deficits. There are presently more than 20 countries

---

[75] Cf. Adams (1995)
[76] Cf. Frantz, Chenut and Walhin (2003)

that run a sovereign wealth fund and six more have expressed interest in starting such a fund. However, the asset holdings of the current funds remains very concentrated, with the top five funds accounting for 70 percent of total assets.[77]

Sovereign wealth funds differ from other funds in such a way that very few of them publish information about their assets, liabilities or investment strategies. Traditionally, sovereign wealth funds are long only, but there is anecdotal evidence that some sovereign funds have placed investments with other leveraged funds.[78] The danger of sovereign funds comes from their sheer size combined with their nebulous actions that have the potential to disrupt international financial markets. In addition, the fact that the funds are government-owned adds the risk that investments are politically motivated and not solely financially or economically driven. Thus, Truman[79] proposes that an international standard on cross-border investments by sovereign wealth funds should cover the topics of objectives and investment strategy, governance, transparency and behavior. Truman[80] also recommends a blueprint for best practices for sovereign wealth funds as suggested by the IMF and OECD. Such a best practice guideline would include factors like structure, governance, accountability and transparency as well as behavior. Truman rates the funds on each of these criterions and ranks them accordingly.

Fotak, Bortolotti and Megginson[81] are among the first to research the impact of sovereign wealth funds on listed companies. They discover that contrary to the public perception, the funds mostly buy minority stakes directly from the targeted companies, roughly half of which are unlisted and in the fund's home country. Another interesting finding shows that around the announcement date of the transaction, there is a 0.8 percent abnormal positive return of the target company's share price. However, two-year abnormal returns of sovereign wealth funds average a significantly negative 14 percent, suggesting that equity acquisitions of sovereign funds are followed by a price deterioration of the target company.

Balding[82] also analyzes portfolios of sovereign wealth funds and develops three key conclusions, which are contrary to the public opinion about these funds. Applying direct and indirect statistics, Balding discovers that estimates on the size of funds are based on inconsistent calculations and thus not reliable. Secondly, he proves his hypothesis that sovereign wealth funds are rational investors, driven by economical and financial impact. In his analysis,

---

77 Cf. Johnson (2007), p56
78 Cf. Johnson (2007), p57
79 Cf. Truman (2007), p7
80 Cf. Truman (2008), p6 et sqq.
81 Cf. Fotak et al. (2008)
82 Cf. Balding (2008)

Balding finds that the funds are diversified by both asset class and geographic region. His third point concerns the impact of sovereign wealth funds on international financial markets. According to Balding, there is little evidence that this impact is negative and thus, there is little need for regulatory restrictions of cross-border investments.

Having summarized the four most relevant types of funds for this thesis, the next chapter will provide an overview over the recent developments of asset management, the impact of the financial crisis and current industry trends.

2.3 Recent Industry Developments

According to Garvey et al., one megatrend of the asset management industry is the shift in saving behavior among retail clients. As they found out in a survey, plans to increase personal savings in the future are widespread among the population.[83]

Another major trend in the industry is the increased importance of ETFs. While in recent years they have mostly been used as passive investment vehicles, they are now set to become the fundamental building blocks of active asset management, specifically for mutual fund management.[84]

For the pension fund industry, 2009 ended in a 13 percent rise of assets in the 13 largest pension fund markets. However, the absolute levels are still below their 2007 values. In terms of pension assets to GDP ratio, the industry is back to its 2003 levels. The global market of pension assets has seen a significant change over the last ten years, with the three largest markets (USA, Japan and UK) each losing share in global pension assets due to a slower growth rate relative to other countries. When comparing DC to DB assets, one can see that the former have grown at a rate of 6.4 percent p.a. over the last years versus a much slower rate of 1.6 percent p.a. for DB assets. The trend shows an established provision towards DC funds, which now make up 42 percent of total pension assets compared to 32 percent in 1999. These values differ substantially between countries, but can be seen in almost all countries with significant pension fund existence. Japan is the only exception by remaining 100 percent DB. Concerning asset allocation, two trends can be identified over the last year: a sizeable shift into equity investments and further diversification of portfolios into alternative assets.[85]

---

[83] Cf. Garvey et al. (2010), p20
[84] Cf. Saluzzi and Hage (2010), p4 et sqq.
[85] Cf. Judd and Yin (2010), p4 et sqq.

The financial crisis that started in 2007 has left its marks on the global asset management industry. The following chapter briefly states the challenges that arise from the crisis and what impact the newly imposed regulations of governments and exchange commissions will have on asset managers.

2.3.1 Aftermath of the Financial Crisis

The principal issues that the financial crisis left with pension funds are diverse across the globe. For the largest pension fund markets, the new challenges include liquidity concerns, the management of credit and collateral risk, the underperformance of asset managers and new challenges in the strategic asset allocation.[86]

Another current issue that surfaced during and after the financial crisis is the exposure of poor governance across the asset management value chain. According to Saluzzi and Hage[87], asset managers as well as intermediaries need to improve their due diligence standards and make clear that effective oversight is part of the value of their services provided.

Sovereign wealth funds were also hit by the financial crisis, with the best performing funds coming from the Middle East and North Africa, where average losses amounted to 20 to 25 percent of the value of the known equity portfolio. These funds, however, played a special role during the crisis: As the crisis unfolded, they initially rushed in to help, pouring billions of dollars into banks in the United States and Western Europe during the winter of 2007–2008. These investments provided liquidity that at first seemed to stabilize uneasy markets. As conditions deteriorated, however, the funds began to retreat from developed-market equities, engage in fewer transactions and invest locally. This was done to both prop up struggling banks and companies and continue development and diversification of their domestic economies.[88]

After the financial crisis, a more pronounced divergence between institutional and retail investment management markets can be observed. According to Seymour et al.[89], this is due to factors such as different investor needs concerning the level of sophistication, knowledge and risk appetite between the investor groups. Another big factor contributing to the divergence phenomenon is the new regulatory landscape after the crisis. Much of the regulation is aimed at the retail market, which forces many smaller asset management firms to go down the institutional route where compliance costs and burdens are less onerous. However, Seymour

[86] Cf. Judd and Yin (2010), p4
[87] Cf. Saluzzi and Hage (2010), p17
[88] Cf. Barbary and Chin (2009), p4
[89] Cf. Seymour et al. (2010), p9

et al. do not expect these developments to be a long-term trend, as the influencing factors driving investment managers' attitudes and behavior today – such as the economic crisis, high-profile fraud cases, the perception of certain types of asset managers contributing to systemic risk and the regulatory changes arising out of these issues – are based on events with a relatively short time frame. As the market situation improves, focus will shift away from regulation back to result-driven performance again.[90]

Stier et al.[91] also discover that the new regulatory environment following the financial crisis is becoming increasingly complex for asset managers and investment companies. Extensive legislation requiring most private fund advisers to register with the SEC, a greater emphasis on enforcement and fraud prevention as well as stringent new tax proposals are combining to create new challenges for mutual fund managers.

2.3.2 Industry Trends

In this chapter, three trends that recently emerged in the asset management industry are presented. These trends include the demand for social, ethical and sustainable investments (SRI) as well as Sharia-conform products. The third trend deals with the lowering of management cost in the industry.

Socially responsible investors are concerned about social, ethical and especially environmental issues in enterprises. They invest mostly with clear mandates to their asset managers to invest responsibly. The idea originally stems from church-related sponsors that demanded their assets not to be placed in certain companies. This negative screening developed into a range of eight strategies that are used and combined to select investment targets.[92] These strategies include ethical inclusions, positive screening of committed companies, best in class per sector, thematic investment propositions, norms-based filtering, simple exclusions, investor engagement and integration by asset managers of corporate governance risk into traditional financial analysis.[93]

The growth rates of assets under management of ethical funds reached double digits at the beginning of the new century and are currently at 15-20 percent per year.[94] Especially in the United States, where pension funds have been facing governance regulations to invest in ethical companies, the percentage of socially responsible investments is large. Similar

---

[90] Cf. Seymour et al. (2010), p11
[91] Cf. Stier et al. (2010), p4
[92] Cf. Figeac (2007), p23
[93] Cf. Eurosif: European SRI Study (2006), p3
[94] Cf. Abdallah et al. (2009), p3

regulations have been passed in the UK and Germany recently. The importance of ethical investing has reached the point where indices that catalyze the growth of assets under management in the field are created to reflect the performance of sustainable, ethical or eco-friendly companies. The strategy that includes ethics, performance and risk in asset management is considered "triple bottom line investing".[95]

Islamic finance is a new area in the field of finance that has emerged in order to serve clients that require products with conformity to Islamic law and is now one of the fastest-growing segments in finance. Among other restrictions, the Sharia prohibits interest on investments as well as gambling, risk and uncertainty. This leaves the Islamic investor with two basic options to manage his funds. He can empower his asset manager to invest funds in conditional or limited investments; that is, specific companies or sectors. The second option is to give the investment manager unconditional authorization to invest in a suitable project. Both investment categories are also compliant with the law that company profits are to be shared among investors.[96] The total number of Sharia-compliant funds is currently estimated at 950. The asset allocation is impacted by Sharia restrictions in a way that the fixed income allocation is reduced whereas the equity and alternative investment allocations are increased. The idea of Islamic finance is not restricted to, but prevails in, the pension fund market of the Cooperation Council for the Arab States of the Gulf (GCC) with estimated AuM of $63 billion. Recently, global mutual funds have picked up on this investment strategy.[97]

In Europe, the asset management industry continues to be an immensely profitable one according to Hoyos-Gomez, Huber and Schachner. However, their study finds that cost margins have increased over the last years, which leaves the risk of setbacks in this cyclical industry. The critical dependence on capital market performance combined with inflexible cost structures of most asset management companies threatens profits. Operating costs have increased especially in sales and marketing as well as fund management over the last few years, which ultimately can lead to a new composition of the competitive market in Europe.[98] The general approach of asset managers to high cost levels in a downward market is to cut discretionary spending and right-sizing. Lately, the activities to cut costs have been less familiar but more constructive. Through product proliferation, the market is flooded with funds that are not necessary or desirable and the consolidation of such funds results in increased efficiency. Remuneration is an additional topic that asset management companies

95 Cf. Schäfer (2001)
96 Cf. Gait and Worthington (2009)
97 Cf. Abdi et al. (2008)
98 Cf. Hoyos-Gomez, Huber and Schachner (2008)

have set focus on recently. Especially in the light of the new regulations on their way to the market that target additional stress testing, liquidity management etc., flexible cost structures are inevitable for investment managers. This also has the potential to change the current market structure, if small asset managers are unable to cope with the new wave of regulation.[99]

3. Asset Management in the International Perspective

After having examined the asset management industry as an executive force of the investment schemes of institutional investors, the following chapter aims at providing insights to differences in legislature and governance of institutional investors between Germany and the United States. Differences in market regulation for pension funds and insurance companies by the authorities, compliance and disclosure standards, fees as well as taxes are highlighted and implications for asset allocation, performance and risk management are derived. These hypotheses will then be tested empirically in the next chapter.

3.1 Legal Environment in Germany and the USA

3.1.1 Investment Regulation

Investment regulation for pension funds and insurances can be done in two alternative approaches, namely prudent person rules and quantitative portfolio restrictions. Both approaches aim at ensuring adequate portfolio diversification and liquidity of the asset portfolio, but are radically different. They are not, however, polar opposites and studies have revealed that there are gradations between the two.

A quantitative portfolio regulation is simply a quantitative limit on holdings of a given asset class. Typically, those instruments whose holding is limited are those with high price volatility and/or low liquidity. For pension funds, there are also often limits on self-investment of the fund in the assets of the sponsoring firm to protect more directly against the risk of insolvency of the sponsor and appearance of conflicts of interest. Meanwhile, self-investment by life insurance companies is generally forbidden. Furthermore, there are commonly restrictions on the proportion of the assets of an investor exposed to a single borrower or piece of real

[99] Cf. Rolt, Young and Lofts (2009)

estate.[100] The focus here is placed on the investment itself and its riskiness is measured instrument by instrument according to a fixed standard.[101]

The prudent person rule is a concept whereby investments are made in such a fashion that they are considered to be managed prudently. Prudently is defined as handling the investments, as one would do in the conduct of his or her own affairs. Often times, the prudent person rule is accompanied by an asset-liability management exercise.[102] The focus here is placed on the behavior of the person concerned and the investment process forms the key test of prudence. It needs to be assessed whether, for example, there has been a thorough consideration of the issues and there is not blind reliance on experts. It is essential to have undertaken a form of due diligence investigation in forming the strategic asset allocation prior to any change or variation to it. The institution is also expected to have a coherent and explicit statement of investment principles.[103]

Until May 2002, there was no single authority supervising the German asset management industry. Based on the Financial Services and Integration Act (FinDAG), the Federal Financial Supervisory Authority (BaFin) was founded by merging the three current supervisory authorities: the Federal Banking Supervisory Office (BAKred), the Federal Supervisory Office for the Securities Trading (BAWe) and the Federal Insurance Supervisory Office (BAV).[104] Among other responsibilities, the BaFin now supervises insurances through the Insurance Supervision Law (VAG), which requires insurance companies to receive and maintain their business approval of the BaFin. The BaFin includes pension and burial funds in their insurance supervision.[105] Pension funds for professionals in private practice in Germany are regulated on state level, generally by the ministry of finance or ministry of the interior. In most cases, the regulators maintain the power of supervision, yet model their regulation on the federal guidelines for insurances, namely §54 VAG in conjunction with §§1-7 AnlV, operationalized by the BaFin in circular letter 15/2005. Exemplary states that are explicitly following the BaFin regulation are North Rhine-Westphalia and Bavaria, arguably the two largest markets for pension funds for professionals in private practice.[106]

100 Cf. Davis (2000), p20
101 Cf. Goldman (2000)
102 Cf. Davis (2000), p20
103 Cf. Goldman (2000)
104 Cf. Franks and Mayer (2001), p124 et sqq.
105 Cf. Prabhakar (2009), p86 et sqq.
106 Cf. VAG NRW §3, VersAufsVO NRW §§6-7, DVVersoG §9

The VAG aims at reaching an adequate allocation and diversification of an insurance's capital investments in order to reach high security and performance while maintaining the company's liquidity at any time.[107] Circular letter 15/2005 prioritizes security of investments and states that bonds and loans have a maximum maturity of twelve years. The cash equivalent of the capital guarantee needs to amount to at least 50 percent of the principal and investments into non-fungible assets that cannot be liquidated at any time are prohibited. This means that e.g. many closed funds are not an investment option for insurance companies. Assets that are rated by the established agencies (Standard & Poor's, Fitch and Moody's) have to show at least investment grade. Where different ratings across agencies occur, the worse rating is pivotal. Exceptions to the latter rule are restricted to assets that show sufficient risk-bearing ability despite their speculative grade rating by one or more of the agencies.[108] Circular letter 15/2005 also specifies the maximum investments into certain asset classes as defined in §2 AnlV. It states that loans on securities may not exceed 5 percent of coverage assets. Similarly, loans given to foreign governments with uncertain or no priority claim may not exceed 10 percent of coverage assets. Asset backed securities and credit-linked notes as well as structured debt securities that possess significant credit risk in addition to their market risk are limited to 7.5 percent of coverage assets. Positions in bonds that are traded outside of the Eurozone must be smaller than 10 percent. Other bonds not yet covered by paragraph V. may not exceed 5 percent of coverage assets. Shares of companies headquartered outside the Eurozone are limited to 10 percent of coverage assets. Investments into hedge funds are restricted to 5 percent of coverage assets. Up to 10 percent of coverage assets may be invested at will upon request to the BaFin.[109] Risky assets, defined as shares, profit participation rights and subordinate debt may not exceed 35 percent of coverage assets.[110] Holdings with limited fungibility may not exceed 10 percent of coverage assets unless the holding company's sole business purpose is stock investments, in which case paragraph V.2.a) takes effect. As for debt investments, up to 10 percent of coverage assets may be invested into risky assets at will upon request to the BaFin.[111] Finally, real estate investments are limited to 25 percent of coverage assets.[112] Furthermore, circular letter 15/2005 states that at least 80 percent of assets have to be invested in the same currency as the insurance company's liabilities, which leaves up to 20 percent of assets to be invested incongruently concerning the liabilities' currency.[113]

[107] Cf. VAG §54 Para. 1
[108] Cf. BaFin (2005): Circular Letter 15/2005 II. 1. a)-d)
[109] Cf. BaFin (2005): Circular Letter 15/2005 V. 1. a)-h)
[110] Cf. BaFin (2005): Circular Letter 15/2005 V. 2. a)
[111] Cf. BaFin (2005): Circular Letter 15/2005 V. 2. e)-f)
[112] Cf. BaFin (2005): Circular Letter 15/2005 V. 3.
[113] Cf. BaFin (2005): Circular Letter 15/2005 VI.

As the AnlV has been renewed in 2010, the BaFin is currently drafting a new circular letter to update the asset allocation limits. The new recommendations are expected to be published in spring 2011.[114]

In the United States, the setting for regulation is a very different one. The 50 states regulate the insurance industry themselves, which through the history of insurance regulation has brought federal-state tensions. However, the National Association of Insurance Commissioners (NAIC), a voluntary association of state insurance commissioners, has played an essential role in the centralization process of insurance regulation. Through the successful work of the NAIC, the single states show a high congruence concerning insurance regulation across the United States.[115] Pensions in the United States are invested on an individual level through the 401(k) retirement savings plan and regulated through the Employee Retirement Income Security Act (ERISA).

Due to investments being made on individual level, the rules for pension fund investments are fairly lax. There are no quantitative restrictions on domestic assets in place and a restriction on foreign asset investments is non-existent. However, the prudent person rule is in place and provides a general requirement for diversification. For defined benefit funds, the self-investment limit is 10 percent whereas there is no limit on self-investment for defined contribution funds.

The life insurance market is regulated on state level, generally through quantitative restrictions. One example is the state of Delaware that limits investments into capital and surplus in shares to 25 percent, investments into real estate to 25 percent and investments into fixed income to 50 percent. New Jersey sets its limits for shares, real estate and loans to 15, 10 and 60 percent respectively. Many states limit the per-issuer exposure of issuers other than the U.S. government to 3-5 percent. Currency matching is not enforced, whereas there is an aggregate 0-10 percent investment restriction on foreign assets.[116] In general, the quantitative limits that many states impose on insurance companies are not as specific and detailed as the counterparts in Germany are and leave more room for the asset managers' investment decisions.

The hypotheses that can be drawn from these different regulation designs are as follows

114 Cf. BaFin (2010a): Circular Letter Draft, reference number VA 54 – I 3200 – 2010/0008
115 Cf. Randall (1999), p629 et sqq.
116 Cf. OECD (2000, 2003) as well as Dickinson (1998)

H1: Portfolios in the United States should exhibit a broader range of allocation fractions within asset classes and

H2: higher variance of allocation among companies, as limits are less strict than in Germany and quantitative restrictions are not imposed, or on a higher level than in Germany.

H3: This could, at times, lead to the dominance of certain asset classes across the whole industry in the US, due to a more liberal strategic and tactical asset allocation and

H4: increase overall portfolio volatility as well as VaR through reduced diversification.[117]

H5: Prudent person rules as used in the United States should result in superior performance of funds compared to strict quantitative restrictions, due to the greater amount of investment opportunities.[118]

H6: Assuming that the quantitative restrictions imposed by German commissioners are efficient, they will reduce the portfolio risk measured by asset depreciation by limiting various exposures, such as to credit risk or concentration risk.

H7: Despite the prudent person rule, one can expect less diversification in pension assets in the United States due to a "naïve diversification" behavioral bias.[119]

H8: The home bias[120] should be overemphasized for insurance investors in both countries compared to non-regulated investors due to limited regulatory tolerance on foreign investments.

3.1.2 COMPLIANCE

Information is required in order to examine whether the German institutional investors comply with the regulations provided by the respective controlling institution (BaFin or a state ministry) – in other words, whether they are capable of identifying, managing and monitoring risks of their investments. Even if the insurance company outsourced at least parts of the investment management and/or risk management, it remains responsible for the provision of this information to the regulators. The German institutional investors have to provide the following information to the BaFin at the end of each calendar year:

- A general description of the intended investment policy and the planned asset portfolio for the current fiscal year, including a depiction of the portfolio risks.
- The current internal investment guidelines for capital investments that highlight changes from the previous year.

---

[117] Cf. Markowitz (1952)
[118] Cf. Davis (2002c)
[119] Cf. Benartzi and Thaler (2001)
[120] Cf. French and Poterba (1991)

- A description of the asset-liability management. Smaller insurances may be exempt from this requirement.

The focus of these reports lies on the changes compared to the previous year. If the latter are of substantial impact, they have to be reported immediately.[121] Regulators of pension funds for professionals in private practice again take a leaf out of the BaFin's book and adopt compliance standards.[122]

As for the compliance of U.S. pension plans, the before-mentioned ERISA plays the most important role. The ERISA is a federal law that sets minimum standards for retirement and health benefit plans in private industry. It does not require any employer to establish a plan; yet those who do establish plans must meet certain minimum standards.[123] Among other things, ERISA demands that those individuals who manage plans (and other fiduciaries) must meet certain standards of conduct. The law also contains detailed provisions for reporting to the government and disclosing to participants. There are provisions aimed at assuring that plan funds are protected and that participants who qualify receive their benefits. Business owners are responsible for ensuring that their 401(k) plans comply with federal law and should rely on other professionals to assist them with their plan duties.[124] ERISA compliance can be divided into three parts. Documentary compliance ensures that the plan and trust documents, summary plan descriptions, employee communication materials and enrollment forms are reviewed to ensure their consistency and compliance. Operational compliance refers to the requirement that the plan is operated in accordance with its written plan documents. Verification must be made so the plans are being operated according to their written terms. Fiduciary compliance includes an analysis made to determine who the fiduciaries are, what their obligations are and what each must do to comply with those obligations.[125]

The quantitative restrictions on investments for insurance companies in the United States are monitored and enforced by the state commissioner of the respective state.

H9: The compliance requirements should have no direct impact on investment behavior, but can partially be measured through expenses occurring to the investor, since in most cases, compliance cost is passed on to the investing institution.[126]

---

[121] Cf. VAG §81 Para. 2, VAG §7 Para. 2, VAG §54d and AnlV §6
[122] Cf. e.g. DVVersoG §11
[123] Cf. ERISA – 29 U.S. Code Chapter 18 Subtitle B Part 5 – Administration and Enforcement
[124] Cf. U.S. Department of Labor (2010)
[125] Cf. Jackson (2007), p28
[126] Cf. e.g. DVVersoG §12, VersAufsVO NRW §4

3.1.3 Disclosure

The disclosure requirements for insurance companies in Germany are regulated through a by-law (RechVersV), in addition to the code of commercial law (HGB). This by-law describes the different design of financial statements as well as details to the valuation rules for actuarial accruals in comparison to other, non-insurance companies.[127] The periodicity of publicity, however, is not affected by the by-law and remains regulated by HGB §325. The latter states that all incorporated companies and registered partnerships without sole proprietors or natural persons as liable partner need to publish financial statements (electronically) within twelve months of the fiscal year.[128] The same rules apply to pension funds in Germany that are also additionally regulated through a by-law (RechPensV). Pension funds for professionals in private practice disclose their information to the respective state regulator.

Insurance companies in the United States have to respond to state law regulation concerning the publication of financial statements. In general, statements have to be made public on a yearly basis in compliance with IAS. The most important standard with regard to the topic of this thesis is IFRS 7. The latter states that insurance companies need to disclose enhanced balance sheet and income statement details by category and class, a liquidity risk maturity analysis showing the remaining contractual maturity for financial liabilities, information relating to the credit quality of financial assets, quantitative disclosures illustrating the sensitivity of profit or loss and company equity to changes in key market risk variables and finally the processes that the company uses to manage and measure risks.[129]

As for the pension plan industry in the United States, companies with a scheme are required to publish annually under IFRS 7 whereas private investors do not disclose their pension investments. However, pension funds are required to summarize information to participants and beneficiaries.[130]

H10: One hypothesis that can be concluded from the disclosure regulation of insurance companies and pension plans is that due to a given choice on how detailed the balance sheet of a German insurance company (or pension fund) needs to be published, a bias might exist where only successful investment results are disclosed and companies may not provide detailed information on failing investments. Compared to the insurance regulation in the United States that meticulously describes the disclosure systematic,

---

[127] Cf. RechVersV Chapter 3, Subchapter 1 §§6-21
[128] Cf. HGB §325 (1)
[129] Cf. IASB: IFRS 7 as well as Ernst & Young (2008)
[130] Cf. ERISA – 29 U.S. Code Chapter 18 Subchapter I Subtitle B Part 1 – Reporting and Disclosure

this might lead to a skew of investment performance of German institutional investors to the better, based on data availability. However, this effect is expected to fade over time since with regulation EC 1606/2002, the European Union has decided that all listed companies should apply the International Financial Reporting Standards for annual accounts starting on or after January 1, 2005. The impacts of this transition on pension schemes have been studied by Swinkels.[131]

3.1.4 Expenses

The expense scheme applied by insurances does not differ between the United States and Germany. Four basic types of expenses are charged to the insurance taker:

- *Administrative expenses* describe the loadings for expenses as a percentage value of the premium. They are traditionally used to cover administrative costs of the insurance company.
- *Collection expenses* are calculated as a percentage value of the premium and traditionally used to finance the cost of premium collection.
- *Additional premium* charges for installments are imputed if the premium is not paid as an annual premium in advance, but rather as monthly installments.
- *Acquisition costs* describe the percentage value of the premium that is used to cover one-time costs such as risk analysis, provisions or other costs of acquisition.

Additional expenses are charged to the insurance taker when the insurance policy is terminated prematurely. Cost of actual asset management is generally not disclosed.

The largest expense blocks are generally administrative and acquisition costs. The average German insurance currently reports administrative expenses of 3.29 percent and acquisition costs of 5.12 percent.[132] In the United States, acquisitions expenses are amortized on a proxy basis, which is referred to as deferred acquisition costs. Based on the specific insurance contract, these can range from 1.75 percent to 7.7 percent.[133]

As for pension funds organized by companies in the United States, a different issue is currently being discussed. The question here is what rules apply to how expenses are allocated among plan participants in a defined contribution pension plan. The two principal issues raised with respect to the allocation of plan expenses in defined contribution plans involve the extent, to which plan expenses are required to be allocated on a pro rata, rather than per

[131] Cf. Swinkels (2007)
[132] Cf. Poweleit (2009)
[133] Cf. Shuster (2009), p4

capita, basis and the extent, to which plan expenses may properly be charged to an individual participant, rather than plan participants as a whole.[134]

H11: The expense structure of insurances and pension funds is not believed to have a significant influence on neither asset allocation, nor performance or risk of the investments as they occur independently of each other.

3.1.5 Taxes

Most insurance companies in Germany are incorporated companies and thus the rules for business tax apply. New tax rates were implemented in 2008 and are as follows: Corporate income tax was reduced from 25 percent to 15 percent jointly with a reduction of the solidarity surcharge. Trade tax was reduced as well while the trade tax multiplier declined to 3.5 percent. This results in a lower average tax encumbrance of 28.65 percent, compared to the previous one of 29.83 percent.[135] Starting in 2009, a flat rate withholding tax of 25 percent was introduced for interest income, dividend income and capital gains income.

Similar to the United States, the academic research in the field of taxation of pension funds on corporate level in Germany is not abundant, as the focus of most taxation literature lies with individual tax. Taxes on capital gains, dividends and interest of pension funds are taxed at the 25 percent flat rate withholding tax.

In the United States, an insurance company's share of net investment income is computed for purposes of determining availability of tax-exempt interest exclusion and dividend-received deduction. While realized net capital gains are included in gross income, special rules apply to dividend income: 80-100 percent owned subsidiary dividends are fully deductible, 20-80 percent owned corporation dividends are eligible for 80 percent deduction and less than 20 percent owned corporation dividends are eligible for 70 percent deduction.[136] Capital taxes and taxes on securities are currently imposed by only a few states.[137] The top federal corporate tax rate is 35 percent, to which state and/or city/county tax might be added. Even though tax rates currently differ depending on the taxable income from 15 percent to 39 percent[138], 35 percent is a standard assumption for the federal U.S. corporation income tax.[139]

---

[134] Cf. Doyle (2003)
[135] Cf. Göttsche (2007)
[136] Cf. Shuster (2009), p5
[137] Cf. Ibid., p6
[138] Cf. U.S. Code, Title 26 (Internal Revenue Code), Subtitle A, Chapter 1, Subchapter A, Part II, Section 11
[139] Cf. Schanz (2009)

As 401(k) plans are most commonly managed on an individual basis, the issues related to taxation take place on this level as well. A company's employees can choose whether their contributions are made on a pre-tax or after-tax basis, yet the earnings from the plan are tax-deferred with either option. Thus, the pension fund can offer a major benefit through the compounding of interest. ERISA benefit plans are subject to federal taxing power.[140] While the progressive tax rate is applied to ordinary income, capital gains and dividends are taxed at a reduced flat rate of 15 percent. Capital gains include both gains on shares and on real estate in the United States.[141]

The implications of tax rates for investment behavior are as follows:

H12: The lower withholding flat tax rates in the United States are not expected to ignite differences to investment behavior compared to Germany, as there is little to no room for investment optimization with respect to taxes in a flat tax regime.

H13: Due to certain reduced capital gains and dividends tax rates for domestic investments in the United States, one can expect a tendency to invest domestically beyond the already existing availability bias as described by Kahneman and Tversky.[142]

H14: A difference between tax rates on long-term investment and short-term investment in the United States should encourage investors to hold on to their assets for at least the required holding period to receive the lower tax rate.

H15: This speculative period was abandoned in Germany in 2009, yet it is probably too early to see implications of reformation in the data.

3.2 Corporate Governance in the Insurance and Pension Fund Industry

Having highlighted the most important external surrounding conditions for insurances and pension funds in Germany and the United States as well as the major differences between the regulations of these two countries, the following chapter aims at providing similar information concerning the internal decision-making processes for institutional investors. Governance plays an important role in this field of asset management due to the principal-agent constellation between sponsors and investors. In this setting, the information asymmetry is paired with incongruent goals of both parties and different levels of risk aversion. This can lead to behavior that is not in the best interest of all parties involved[143], such as window dressing as mentioned in chapter 2.2.1, and thus many companies specifically state their

140 Cf. ERISA - 29 U.S. Code Chapter 18 Subchapter I Subtitle A - General Provisions
141 Cf. Schanz (2009)
142 Cf. Kahneman and Tversky (1974)
143 Cf. Spatt (2005)

stance on and policy for corporate governance. Corporate governance generally provides a system with which a company is able to govern itself. The system defines roles, responsibilities as well as accountabilities and is defined by five constituents[144]:

- *Corporate culture and environment* including values, ethics, ease with which employees raise concerns or report irregularities, etc.
- *Corporate structures* including board of directors, senior management, business area functions, etc.
- *Essential governing documents and policies* including by-laws, organizational rules, committee mandates etc.
- *Strategies, policies, procedures and controls* covering risks to which the insurer is exposed and risk management, compliance, audit, financial reporting, etc.
- *Decision-making and actions* linked to this culture, environment and framework of structures, policies and controls.

3.2.1 Best Practices for the Insurance Industry

Despite the fact that there is no legal requirement to do so, there has been a recent drive within the non-public company sector of the insurance industry to adopt certain corporate governance best practices as set forth in the Sarbanes-Oxley Act of 2002 and the various securities exchanges.[145] The increased attention led the International Association of Insurance Supervisors (IAIS) to adopt revised Insurance Core Principals (ICPs) and an associated Assessment Methodology, offering new guidance for the effective operation of supervisory systems around the world in 2003. The assistance provided by the IAIS captures corporate governance for both insurance companies and insurance supervision.[146] Extending the frameworks set up over the years, the IAIS released a joint issues paper with the OECD in pursuit of enhancing the protection of policyholders and shareholders beyond the system already provided by existing regulation and supervision as well as developing guidance specifically directed to the insurance sector that would supplement corporate governance rules generally applicable to non-insurance companies.

According to the IAIS and OECD[147], corporate governance for the insurance industry covers seven different topics:

144 Cf. IAIS and OECD (2009), p11
145 Cf. English et al. (2005), p2
146 Cf. International Association of Insurance Supervisors (2003)
147 Cf. IAIS and OECD (2009), p9 et sqq.

- Governance structures define the role of the board in setting strategies and policies as well as overseeing senior management. The different functions of the board are delegated to board committees, such as an audit, a compensation and a corporate governance committee.[148] The composition of the board itself is governed with the help of proper criteria for executive and non-executive members. Furthermore, the board needs to show independence of decision-making.
- The functions of the board include the setting of strategies and policies as well as delegating and reporting. The board is supposed to take on responsibilities in the areas of corporate governance, ethics and business conduct as well as conflicts of interest. A major governance function of the board includes the remuneration and possible perverse incentives leading to unacceptable risk taking of decision-makers. It is the board's responsibility to ensure adequate qualifications and training of board members. Defining the extent to which accountability is shared between the board and executive managers is also a function of the board.
- The control functions of corporate governance include risk management, compliance, internal audit and other control functions as an integral element of a sound governance system. This includes dealing with solvency issues of the company related to corporate governance, such as internal modeling, stress testing etc. The use of external rating agencies is to be determined as well as the staffing and independence of internal control functions.
- The qualifications and independence of actuarial functions and auditors has to be determined.
- The disclosure of corporate governance has to be developed in terms of transparency.
- The relationship with stakeholders must be managed adequately, where the participating policyholders form a special class of stakeholder. The responsibility of an insurance company towards society is governed through corporate social responsibility.
- Effective corporate governance can assist the supervisor by making it possible for the supervisor to have greater confidence in the work and judgment of an insurer's board, senior management and control functions. This contributes to the supervisor's ability to protect policyholders' interests.

3.2.2 Best Practices for Pension Funds

The Investment Governance Group (IGG) identifies three steps on a pension fund's way to good investment governance, which is the heart of a well-run scheme. First, roles and respon-

148 Cf. English et al. (2005), p6

sibilities in relation to investment decision-making and governance should be clearly defined and communicated to stakeholders. Second, informed choice is at the heart of effective decision-making – monitoring and communicating investment performance can help members to achieve better returns. Finally, appropriate investment options have to be available to suit members' diverse profiles and needs – even where members choose to remain inactive.[149]

According to Clark and Urwin, there is increasing evidence to support a link between superior investment performance and an institutional investor's strong governance. Many pension funds are beginning to realize that their governance arrangement should be a top priority, not only because of the responsibility to literally millions of individuals, but also because it constitutes an opportunity for wealth creation. At the same time, it is important to point out that while strong governance is hugely important in institutional investment, it is a very difficult area to get right, with only the most conscientious and gifted companies succeeding in all areas.[150]

Urwin[151] identifies the six best governance practices for pension funds that lead to organizational excellence and effectiveness:

- *Investment Executive*: The merits of separating governance into a governing function and an executive function cannot be understated. The former sets the framework, monitors and controls, while the latter makes the decisions within the given framework and implements them. Not only does this improve efficiency and accountability, but it also allows for the concentration of investment expertise within the executive function. Best practice funds adopt a clear separation of governing and executive functions with a strong culture of accountability. Furthermore, the executive function has a high level of investment competency, enabling the funds to implement and monitor complex investment arrangements.
- *Board Selection and Competence*: Sound investment competencies are also observed at the board level of best practice funds. Board members ideally have strong numeric skills and the ability to think logically within a probability-based domain; such skills enable the board to function effectively in its long-horizon mission.
- *Supportive Compensation*: Leading funds address this at both the board and executive level with some success at using compensation to attract appropriate skills and align actions to the goals of the fund. Current practice among funds in general appears to re-

[149] Cf. IGG (2010)
[150] Cf. Clark and Urwin (2007)
[151] Cf. Urwin (2008)

sult in significantly higher payments to external board members and executives. There is scope to address this imbalance through greater use of internal resources – an approach that is becoming more widely adopted.

- *Competitive Advantage*: Investment is a highly competitive activity and, for funds to succeed, they need to be aware of their competitive advantages and disadvantages and adapt their decision-making accordingly. Much of their competitive advantage will be built on a sound belief structure, but will also maximize their own particular areas of competence. It is equally important that funds should be aware of areas where they have no expertise and seek to limit their strategy accordingly.
- *Real-Time Decisions*: Most funds are geared towards making decisions around a calendar-based series of meetings. Best practice funds, however, tend to have processes in place that enable decisions to be made when necessary, based on investment market conditions. Making such a change from calendar to real-time focus involves more delegation and a clear definition of responsibilities.
- *Learning Organization*: Best practice funds tend to be more innovative than other funds. To be successful, they need to operate in a culture that learns from experience. They also need to be willing to challenge conventional wisdom and deal enthusiastically with change.

H16: According to Clark and Urwin [152] as well as Ambachtsheer, Capelle and Scheibelhut[153], the organizational design of a pension fund and its degree of congruence with the best practices mentioned are decisive factors for fund performance. Pension funds with exemplary corporate governance should outperform those who lack adequate rules for internal decision-making.

Besides the many regulation and governance factors with influence on investment behavior mentioned in this chapter, there are still numerous other influencing parameters left. Instead of trying to list and describe these in a generalistic manner, the ones important for this thesis are evaluated where useful over the course of chapter 4.3. The following chapter summarizes the interviews conducted in the course of this study to provide an insight perspective of experts and practitioners dealing with investment regulation and corporate governance on a daily basis.

152 Cf. Clark and Urwin (2007)
153 Cf. Ambachtsheer, Capelle and Scheibelhut (1998)

3.3 Practitioner's Perspective on the Impact of Regulation and Governance

Even though the goals of investment regulation stated in §54 VAG are generalistic and blurry, the German regulators do not see a need to quantify them in terms of a maximal portfolio volatility or capital depreciation quota. Consequently, the process to determine quantitative limits for investments and asset allocation is not very surprising; instead of empirically modeling such limits for institutional investors to ensure a reduction of risk, the barriers have historically grown to where they are now. If new asset classes are approved by regulators, the limits are set precautiously low. While the BaFin shows that the industry is not operating near the restrictions currently set[154], it remains unclear as to whether this is a natural behavior by investors or whether the investment quotas are pushed down artificially through the quantitative limits. Compared to prudent person rules, the system employed in Germany yields advantages such as clear demarcation, simplified communication between the regulator and investors as well as ensured diversification of assets.

From the practitioners' perspective, the general attitude towards investment regulation in Germany is positive, due to the provided advantages and the necessity of regulation in the light of the financial crisis. The advantages for asset managers are mostly indirect ones that affect the whole industry in general rather than single organizations. However, the investors feel that the current strictness of the German regulation is not essential, as investment organizations take similar matters into their own hands by developing investment guidelines, risk manuals etc. If the current trend continues, it is likely that the quantitative limits of the BaFin will turn into a real handicap for investors. Further drawbacks of the regulation include the additional expenses for compliance through an increase in personnel or risk systems that need to be established in the investment process. The prudent person rule in the United States does not explicitly require companies to comply with quantitative standards, yet institutional investors believe that their US equivalents restrict themselves with reasonable internal rules that have a similar effect. [155]

Concerning corporate governance, the German market for pension funds for professionals in private practice is still in a very early state. The first governance code was developed by the pension fund for financial auditors in 2007 and contains a code of ethics, including the requirements for investment counterparts, as well as rules of conduct for employees and the need for ethical and sustainable investments. The code, which was developed with external help, received great attention from the institutional peers in Germany and is believed to be

154 Cf. BaFin (2010b), p94

155 Whole paragraph confer discussions with two representatives of large German institutional investors

adopted by large parts of the industry over the next years. Besides governance of the investment process, practitioners impose restrictions towards the actual investments on themselves by establishing the need to predominantly invest in SRI. The range of internal rules for SRI investments reaches from a total ban of investments in certain industries to a best-in-class approach, which means that the company with the highest SRI-fit in the industry can be targeted despite the industry's non-SRI nature.[156]

4. Empirical Examination of International Differences

Having discussed the theoretic foundations of asset management in the setting of institutional investors, the following empirical part of this thesis will examine the practical differences in investment behavior between institutional investors in the United States and Germany. After providing an overview of the differences in asset allocation, investment performance and risk management, the results of this analysis will be investigated in order to find significant drivers of the differences. Finally, conclusions to investment regulation and corporate governance will be drawn and the hypotheses derived in chapter 3 will be evaluated.

4.1 Description of Data Basis and Mathematical Approach

The empirical examination conducted for this thesis aims at identifying differences in investment behavior of institutional investors in the United States and Germany. The analysis is conducted at the highest possible level of institutional investors, namely the fund sponsors. Over the last five years, an average of 137 insurance companies of the United States and 14 insurance companies of Germany have published sufficient data for the analysis each year. This covers the public U.S. market almost completely and around 76 percent of funds of the regulated German insurance and pension market according to numbers provided by the BaFin. In the pension market, the study additionally includes an average of 10 pension funds for professionals in private practice each year for Germany where the data is taken directly from annual reports. Besides this primary data, the study makes use of 401(k) data collected by the Employee Benefit Research Institute (EBRI). Their extensive database provides information of 45.2 percent of 401(k) assets under management over the last five years. The total amount of capital investments analyzed in this study amounts to $27.59 trillion.

Capital investment data for insurance companies was extracted from Factset and annual company reports. In the asset allocation analysis, three asset classes are considered – equity, fixed income and other securities. Equity includes common and non-redeemable preferred

[156] Cf. Ibid.

stock. Fixed income represents investments in fixed income securities such as bonds and redeemable preferred stocks. Other investments include all other investments of the insurance company.

The statistical analysis performed in chapter 4.2 is based on descriptive statistics. Investment risk is measured in terms of depreciation of investments and is also approximated through portfolio volatility and value at risk based on the portfolio's asset allocation. In order to do so, data from S&P, Deutsche Börse, Fidelity Brokerage Services and Hypoport are used. The performance measurement puts the investment income of an insurance company in relation to its total investments.

In order to analyze the results in chapter 4.3, in particular the performance and risk measured by depreciation, statistical regressions are conducted. The principal component regression (PCR) method is used in order to utilize the accessible data adequately. This is necessary due to a previous normalization of absolute investments into asset allocation quotas. According to Mevik and Wehrens, PCR is useful in situations where there are many, possibly correlated, predictor variables and relatively few samples. Instead of regressing the independent variables directly, a principal component analysis (PCA) is performed first by orthogonal transformation in order to identify the components that have high variance without correlation. These principal components are then used as independent variables for the regression. The regressions are run with the pls package in R, which is available from the Comprehensive R Archive Network (CRAN).[157] For explicit explanation of the algorithms used in PCR and the implementation in R, please refer to chapter 1.1 et sqq. of Mevik and Wehrens.[158] The statistical significance of the obtained results is tested with F-statistics.

4.2 Results of Statistical Analysis

Having provided necessary information on the data used in the analyses and having explained the executed procedures, the following chapter presents the results of the descriptive statistics analysis.

[157] Cf. R Development Core Team (2008)
[158] Cf. Mevik and Wehrens (2007)

4.2.1 Asset Allocation

Looking at the asset allocation of insurance companies in the United States and Germany, one can see a similar picture at first glance. Over the last five years, the allocation to fixed income investments has taken up the majority of funds in both countries. The average allocation ranges from 75 percent to 85 percent in the USA and from 69 percent to 89 percent in Germany. In total, US insurance companies invested an average of 80.37 percent into fixed income assets, compared to78.71 percent for German companies. One can further identify a trend in both countries that led to a decrease in the fixed income allocation from 2005 to 2007, followed by a steep increase in the next two years. While the first part of this trend may be attributed to the attractiveness of other asset classes during this time, the sharp reverse in the trend may at large be due to the financial crisis and its impact on risk appetite of institutional investors.

A difference in investment behavior shows in the allocation to equities and other investments. While the equity investments in the United States remain stable between 4 and 5 percent, the quota is highly volatile and at a much higher level in Germany, ranging from 8 percent to 19 percent. The same trend as mentioned for fixed income securities can be seen mirrored in equity investments, especially in Germany. During the first three years of the analysis, the quota is steadily increased until the financial crisis hits and the average allocation to equities in the market is cut in half. Similar results are obtained from the analysis of allocation to other assets. For this asset class, the US investors appear more aggressive in general with a range from 12 to 20 percent, while German investors are more reserved with average quotas of 3 to 12 percent.

The development of asset allocations from 2005 (right) to 2009 (left) is depicted in Figure 6 where blue marks fixed income investments, red marks equity investments and green marks other investments.

Figure 6: Asset Allocation of Insurance Companies between 2005 and 2009

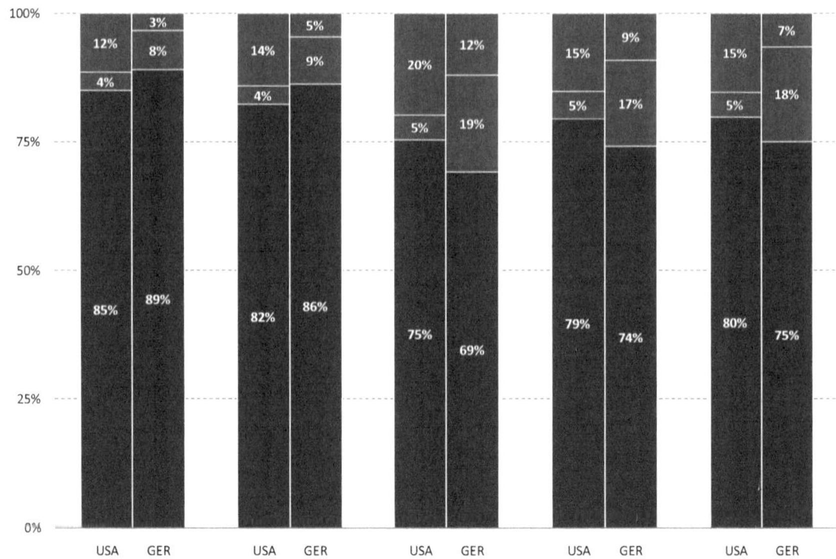

Source: Own calculations

The picture changes drastically when looking at the allocation of pension funds instead of insurance companies. As Figure 7 indicates, little common ground can be found for the asset allocation of 401(k) funds in the United States and that of pension funds for professionals in private practice in Germany. The situation is also different from that just described for insurance companies. While there is no clear dominant asset class for investors in Germany, US investors clearly favor equity investments as they range from 55 to 67 percent of all assets invested. US equity investments are higher than the German equivalent in any observed year, whereas the opposite is true for fixed income investments except for in 2005.

While a similar trend for fixed income and equity investments as mentioned for insurance companies can be seen for pension investments in the US, the pattern in Germany is surprisingly different. After a sharp decline of equity investments after 2005, the quota remains relatively constant around 40 percent, whereas the fixed income proportion steadily increases without obvious catalyzation through the financial crisis.

Figure 7: Asset Allocation of Pension Funds between 2005 and 2009

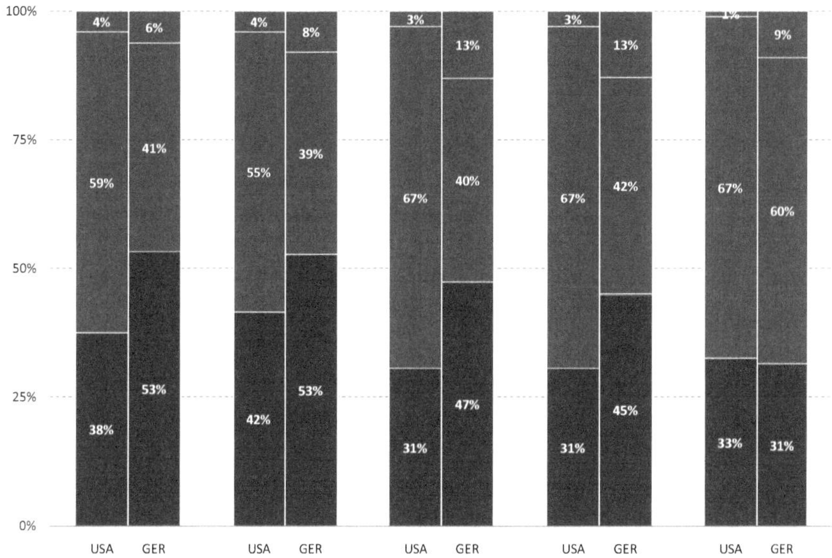

Source: Own calculations

The large difference in other investments between the countries can be explained through the systematical differences in investing for pension funds. While the German pension funds for professionals in private practice generally invest parts of their assets into real estate, the latter is not an option for many investors in the United States as the pension plans offered by the company rarely include elaborated options to invest in other assets than fixed income and equity. However, the trend indicates that other investments, such as real estate as well as "newer" investment options, such as hedge funds or commodities, are becoming more popular. The trend in Germany is clearly dominated by the development of real estate prices that led to a decline in allocation to other assets after the crisis due to both the price effect as well as a change in investment behavior. The tables with detailed data of the asset allocation analysis can be found in Appendix 1.

4.2.2 Risk

Three different risk measures are used to compare the risk management of institutional investors between the United States and Germany. First, depreciation, as it appears in a company's income statement, is taken as a proxy for realized risk taken with the company's capital investments. As depreciation of fixed assets are expected to be very small in comparison to the depreciation of capital assets in the insurance industry, this measure can serve the thesis' purpose on a practical level. Second, the company-specific asset allocation is used to replicate the company's portfolio and calculate the portfolio's volatility. Finally, the same logic is applied to calculate the historical daily value at risk of each company's portfolio at the 99 percent level.

Depreciation is normalized by dividing the company's depreciation by the total amount of investments in fixed income, equity and other capital assets. This depreciation quota is comparable among companies and countries independent of their size or asset allocation.

shows the development of the depreciation quota from 2005 (right) to 2009 (left) for insurance companies in the United States and Germany.

With a mean of 0.89 percent, the average depreciation quota of assets in the United States is 30 times as high as that of German investors. The average values range from 0.79 percent in 2005 to 1.01 percent in the crisis year 2008. The respective values for Germany are 0.02 percent and 0.05 percent where surprisingly the lowest value is measured in 2008 and the highest one in 2009. This leads to the conclusion that depreciation is drawn up in the balance sheet different between the countries, with a more direct impact in the U.S. and a time lag in Germany. The depreciation quota's standard deviation among companies is naturally higher in the U.S. than in Germany due to the higher absolute values of the quota. The spikes of the standard deviation in 2006 and 2008 indicate that in these two years the sheep were separated from the goats in terms of risk management. The same applies to German asset managers for the year 2009 where again we observe a lag in the data in tune with the actual depreciation quota. Despite minor fluctuations, the depreciation quota appears to be comparatively stable in both countries. For the pension fund industry, this measure cannot be calculated due to a lack of data for the American market. However, in Germany the pension funds for professionals in private practice show an average depreciation quota of 0.54 percent with a standard deviation of 0.69 percent. One can see that the range of quotas between 0.10 percent and 1.60 percent is in-between that of insurance companies with the exception of 2008. The same applies to the standard deviation of the quota. The culmination in 2008, however, appears extreme, which can lead to the conclusion that risk management among portfolio managers highly differed that year.

Figure 8: Depreciation Quota of Insurance Companies and VWs from 2005 to 2009

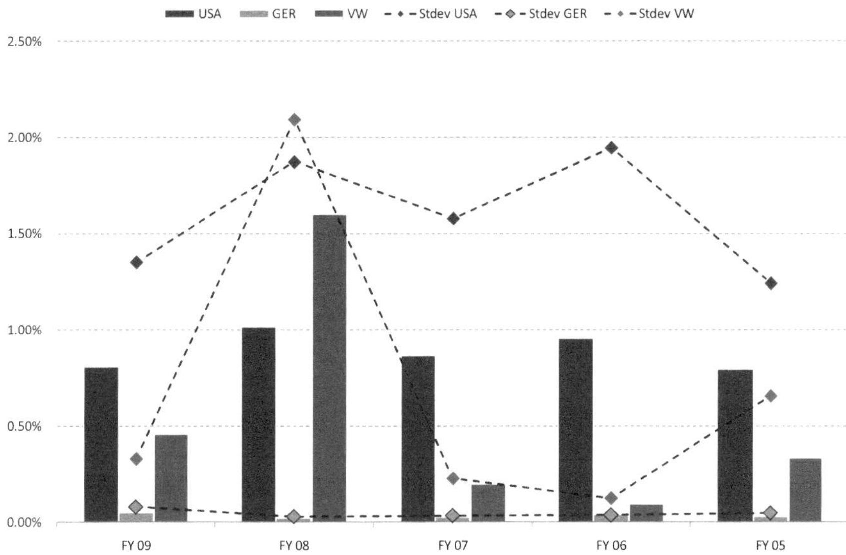

Source: Own calculations

The German BaFin mentions quantitative limits for market risk as essential for insurance companies and pension funds. Such limits can be imposed as VaR or portfolio volatility limits.[159] In accordance with modern portfolio theory as described by Markowitz[160], portfolio variance in a three-asset portfolio is measured by the following formula:

$$\sigma^2 = w_A^2\sigma_A^2 + w_B^2\sigma_B^2 + w_C^2\sigma_C^2 + 2w_Aw_B\sigma_A\sigma_B\rho_{AB} + 2w_Aw_C\sigma_A\sigma_C\rho_{AC} + 2w_Bw_C\sigma_B\sigma_C\rho_{BC}$$

Under the assumption that investors invest all assets of one asset class into a market index, the three assets weights of a portfolio represent the weight of the respective index. In this analysis, the indices are chosen in a way to reflect both a broad market to account for diversification as well as the availability bias as described by Kahneman and Tversky[161]. The U.S. indices used are the S&P 500 for equities, the Fidelity U.S. Bond Index for fixed income and the S&P/Case-Shiller Home Price Index for other assets. The German indices are DAX 30 for equities, RDax for fixed income and the HPX for other assets.

depicts the development of portfolio volatility and its standard deviation across the analyzed insurance companies.

[159] Cf. BaFin (2009): Circular Letter 3/2009 7.3.1 Nr. 8
[160] Cf. Markowitz (1952)
[161] Cf. Kahneman and Tversky (1974)

Figure 9: Projected Volatility of Insurance Companies from 2005 to 2009

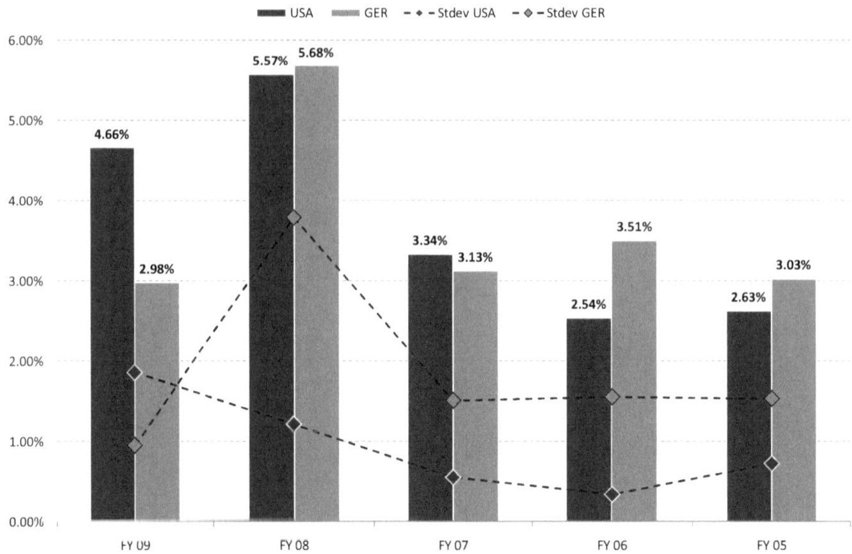

Source: Own calculations

While the average portfolio volatility over the observation period does not differ much between the United States (3.75 percent) and Germany (3.67 percent), the standard deviation within the countries differentiates the two. Except for the year 2009, the standard deviation of German insurance companies is always significantly higher than that of the American equivalents, with the latter being surprisingly low. Investors in both countries experienced an increase in volatility in the crisis year 2008. While the German asset managers have been able to adjust their risk in such a way that the volatility in the following year went back to its original level, volatility remains at a high level in the United States. The trend also shows that standard deviation of volatility among insurance companies in the U.S. has been rising over the last years which points to an increased differentiation among asset managers. As with depreciation, the pattern shows a spike in standard deviation during the crisis in Germany, with the difference that volatility does not lag by a year.

For a given portfolio, probability and time horizon, value at risk is defined as a threshold value such that the probability that the mark-to-market loss on the portfolio over the given time horizon exceeds this value in the given probability level.[162] In this analysis, it is calculated on daily returns at the 99 percent level for each insurance portfolio. Thus, it indicates the

162 Cf. Jorion (2001)

level that a daily portfolio return can range below with the historic probability of one percent. As with the volatility calculation, the assets invested in are assumed the same among all insurances. The results of the analysis are depicted in Figure 10.

Figure 10: Projected Daily VaR at 99% of Insurance Companies from 2005 and 2009

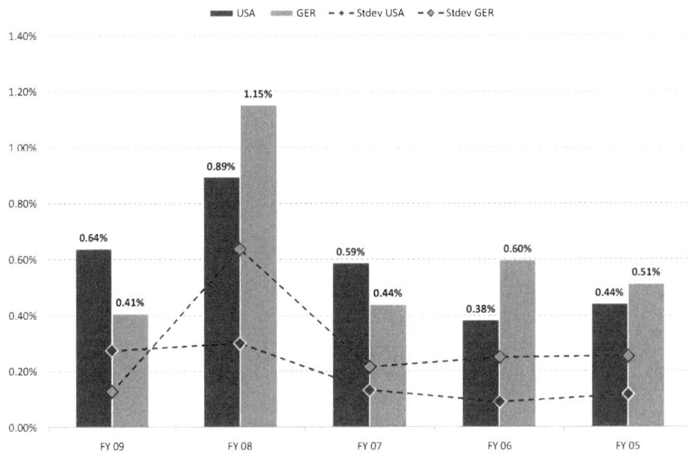

Source Own Calculations

The picture the VaR analysis shows is very similar to that of the volatility analysis. The average VaR is not highly distinguished between the US (0.59 percent) and Germany (0.62 percent). The pattern is also very similar with a relatively stable development from 2005 to 2009 and a spike in the crisis year 2008. The projected values in the United States range from 0.38 percent to 0.89 percent and those of Germany from 0.41 to 1.15 percent. The standard deviation in Germany is consistently higher than in the US except for in 2009. Appendix 1 summarizes the results of the risk management analysis.

4.2.3 Performance

As mentioned in chapter 4.1, the performance measurement divides investment income by total capital assets as published in the insurance companies' financial statements. The measure is calculated for insurance companies in both countries as well as for pension funds for professionals in private practice in Germany. The results of the analysis are shown in Figure 11.

Figure 11: Investment Return of Insurance Companies and VWs from 2005 to 2009

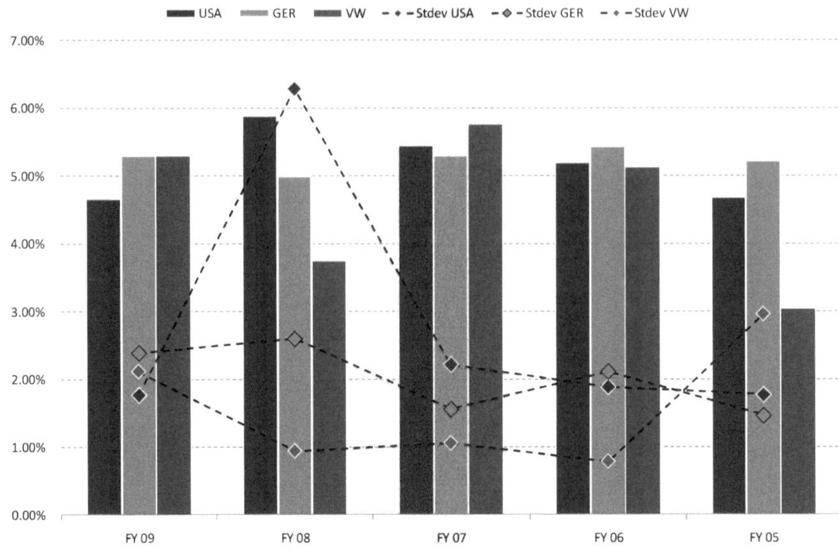

Source: Own calculations

In the insurance industry, neither country's portfolios are dominated by the other; however, returns in Germany appear less volatile than those in the United States. The range of investment performance in the USA reaches from 4.66 percent to 5.88 percent and that of Germany from 4.99 percent to 5.43 percent. On average, German insurance companies achieved a return of 5.25 percent on their capital investments, compared with 5.16 percent for American insurances. The development of returns during the crisis is highly surprising. While in 2008, returns of German insurance companies and especially those of pension funds for professionals in private practice diminished, US investors were actually able to perform better than in any previous year. However, their return in 2009 declined, while German companies were able to recover from the drop in investment income. Once more, the crisis also enhanced the standard deviation between company investment returns in both countries, with the one in the United States almost tripling in 2008. Thus, the crisis certainly took its toll on many investors, while others appear to have been well prepared and able to actually benefit from the crisis. The standard deviation in non-crisis years does not differ significantly between the countries.

Pension funds for professionals in private practice in Germany show even higher return fluctuations than American insurance companies, with average returns ranging from 3.04 percent to 5.76 percent. Surprisingly, 2005 yielded the lowest returns for these funds, in conjunction with a simultaneous maximum in standard deviation among portfolios. The development in 2008, where returns once more dropped from their peak, but standard deviation did not increase, is also noteworthy. This implies that the separation of the wheat from the chaff, as we have seen it in almost all other analyses, did not take place for this investor group in the crisis; they conjointly performed far worse than the year before.

The investment performance analysis is summarized in Appendix 1.

4.3 Analysis of Results

After presenting the results of the various analyses conducted on differences concerning asset allocation, risk management and performance of institutional investors between the United States and Germany, the following chapter aims at analyzing these results. Underlying reasons for the shown differences are examined and hypotheses drawn in chapter 3 are tested.

4.3.1 Asset Allocation

The prudent person rules in place for companies in the United States, as opposed to the strict quantitative restrictions that German institutional investors face, should lead to a more diverse allocation of assets. While this might not be seen directly in the conducted analysis due to a low granularity of asset classes, it could still be observed when looking at the average percentage allocated to an asset class. For this analysis, 10 categories are used to classify the investment quota of each asset class. The average investment percentage across the three asset classes is then assigned to the respective basket, resulting in the histograms depicted in Figure 12.

The first observation is that 0-10 percent bracket in the United States is used by around 15 percent more investors than in Germany on average. Both countries exhibit a trough in the categories ranging from 20-80 percent, yet the American investors appear to rarely use these buckets at all. The two brackets with investment quotas above 80 percent again receive increased attention in both countries. Overall, the allocation in Germany appears to be more diverse than in the United States.[163] In addition to this general conclusion, the differences within a country, but across the observation period, are larger for German investors than for the US counterparts, where little variance can be found over the years. This points to more flexible adjustments of the allocation in Germany. Relating it to the crisis, this statement is strengthened through the data shown in Figure 6, where the shift in allocation during and following the crisis is more severe than that of the United States (e.g. an increase of fixed income allocation of 17 percentage points compared to 7 in the USA).

[163] The average quadratic deviation from the uniform distribution amounts to 2.07% for the United States and 1.35% for Germany.

Figure 12: Average Percentage Allocated to an Asset Class in the US and Germany

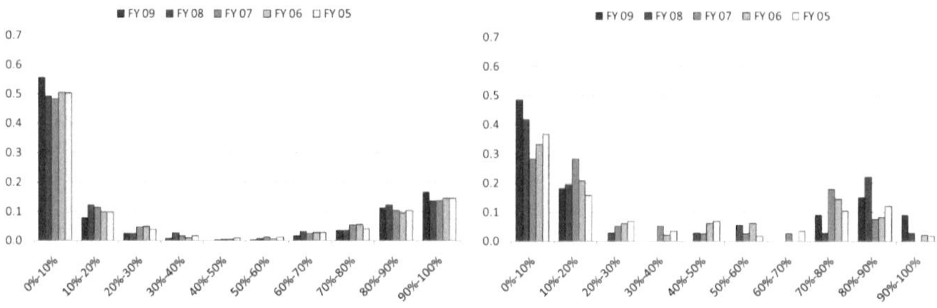

Source: Own Calculations

The asset allocation analysis in chapter 4.2.1 uncovers significant differences in investment behavior between the USA and Germany. However, it is not with gravitas that these differences stem from differences in regulation and/or corporate governance. The asset allocation, particularly the strategic allocation, is influenced by the economic outlook that investors are facing. Often times, especially in large investment institutions, the economic research department plays a vital role in the determination of the strategic allocation. Differences in economic outlooks on both an institutional level as well as a geographical one can ultimately lead to differences in the realized asset allocation. The predominant attitude towards future economic development in the industry can vastly differ between the two countries and therefore impact the strategic allocation. The risk tolerance of the institutional investor is a related aspect that enters the equation. For smaller institutions where investment decisions are made rather on an individual basis than in investment councils, other factors can influence the asset allocation, such as the reputation that an asset class carries. The asset manager himself has a vital impact on the asset selection. His experience as well as his personal risk tolerance and incentive scheme can dominate his decision-making. Considering the leeway that many managers enjoy, especially towards the tactical asset allocation, these traits and circumstances should not be neglected.

For pension investments in the United States, other factors are dominant in the asset allocation decision. Investors frequently choose the path of least resistance by choosing their plan's default options, which often times has an adverse impact on the investor's capital.[164] In addition to this effect, the information overload that many investors in the US are faced with leads to resignation and reduced effort to make the right investment choice.[165] Thus, a large

[164] Cf. Choi et al. (2002)
[165] Cf. Payne (1996) and Agnew and Szykman (2005), p60

share of the asset allocation decision lies with the pension plan providers. The "naïve diversification" bias has a similar quintessence as the path of least resistance phenomenon.

4.3.2 RISK

In order to analyze whether portfolio risk measured by depreciation is driven by asset allocation, a principal component regression is conducted as described in chapter 4.1. The independent variables of this regression are the equity quota, the fixed income quota and the other assets quota of a certain fiscal year of a company. The dependent variable is the company's depreciation quota published in the same report. It is arguable that since asset allocation is an observation at a point of time and depreciation is accumulated over one year, there might be the need for a lag of variables. Thus, in addition to the results shown here, additional regression analyses were conducted where the depreciation of the fiscal year following a published asset allocation was the dependent variable. The results of these regressions are – not surprisingly – very similar to the ones obtained in the original analysis since the date at which the balance sheet is constructed, is independent of accumulated depreciations up to this point, as long as the reporting period remains the same.

depicts the multiple R^2 of the original principal component regressions.

Surprisingly, there is a large difference between the variation of the depreciation that can be explained with the principal component regression between the United States and Germany. While the R^2 in the United States is extremely low with an average of 0.03, asset allocation appears to have a much higher impact on depreciation in Germany, where the average R^2 amounts to 0.42. When looking only at the statistically significant R^2 values, these numbers increase to 0.08 and 0.67 respectively. This extreme difference between the two countries leads to the conclusion that other factors with impact on depreciation are far more important in the US than they are in Germany. Figure 14 exemplarily shows the validation plots that picture the measured depreciation quotas to the ones predicted by the principal component regression for 2006.

Figure 13: Multiple R^2 of PCR with Depreciation as Independent Variable

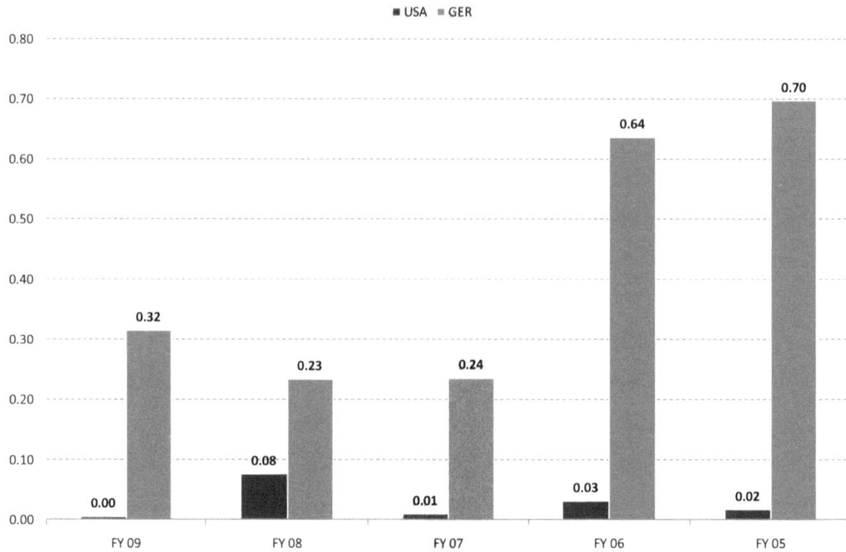

Source: Own Calculations

Figure 14: Principal Component Regression Validation Plots, Depreciation FY 2006

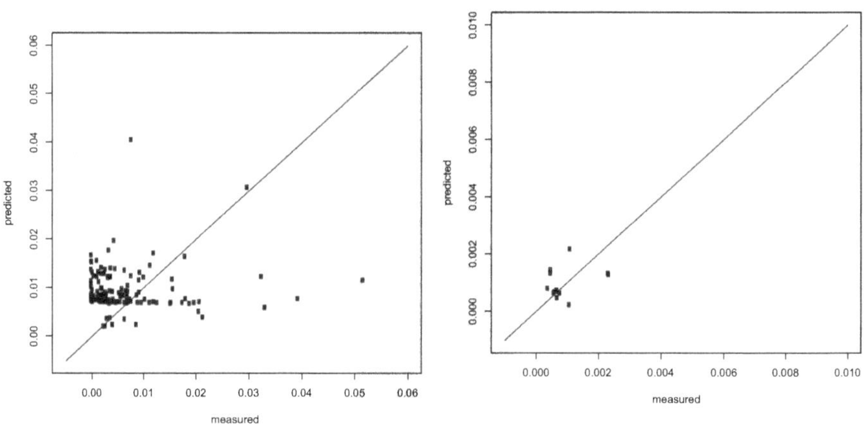

Source: Own Calculations

The plots provide an overview of the data used for the PCR in this year. 26 observations enter the regression for Germany (right) compared to 146 for the United States (left). This already constitutes a statistical explanation for the vast difference in the determination coefficient. An intuitive conclusion from component regression for 2006.

Figure 13 and Figure 14 is that the risk measured by the depreciation quota is easier to control through asset allocation in the German regulation setting than in the US setting. This can be due to the implementation of quantitative restrictions compared to the prudent person rule.

However, a large part of the depreciation quota variation, especially in the US, cannot be explained by the asset allocation alone. The factors that influence depreciation and differences in the latter between both countries are manifold. Once again, the portfolio manager and his unique skill set and traits concerning experience, personal risk preference, his incentive scheme as well as the governance he faces are crucial factors for realized risk in terms of depreciation. Systematic differences between the countries could stem from a different definition of depreciation in the balance sheet. The depreciation data does not always only reflect capital investment depreciation, and the ratio of the latter to fixed asset depreciation can be systematically different between the countries. Also, the way that insurance and pension funds for professionals in private practice are audited can lead to differences. The applied accounting standards can differ between single companies and systematically between the countries. Another systematic difference can be based on different geographical investment focuses. If a large part of investors of one of the countries is focusing its investments in a certain region, whereas investors of the other countries diversify geographically, different economic circumstances impact the portfolio and consequently the depreciation. The country with diversifying investors will thus face very different depreciation quotas in a similar asset allocation, which can lower the coefficient of determination.

For both the volatility and value at risk analyses, the crucial assumption is that asset allocation is the only factor introducing differences between the countries. The analyses leave out company and manager-specific variations of funds and imply that a certain asset allocation leads to a specific risk. This assumption holds on an aggregated level when the sample size is large enough. As mentioned in chapter 2.1.3, it is elemental that some managers outperform the market and others underperform the market, while the average performs with the market. Thus, implying a market portfolio for the average institutional investors of a country in the analyses can reveal differences between the two countries. The numbers computed in the calculations, however, should be used as ballpark figures rather than hard facts, since for simplicity reasons, the availability bias is exaggerated in the process.

4.3.3 Performance

The regression conducted to research the impact of asset allocation on fund performance follows the same procedure as that for depreciation. The only difference lies with the dependent variable that is now measured as investment income divided by total investment. The analysis is run with the accumulated investment income for one period and the asset allocation at the end of this period. Lagging returns by one year, so that the asset allocation at the beginning of the recorded year is used as independent variables, again shows no major deviations from the results, as expected. The coefficients of determination of the analysis for both countries over the years are shown in Figure 15.

Figure 15: Multiple R^2 of PCR with Investment Performance as Independent Variable

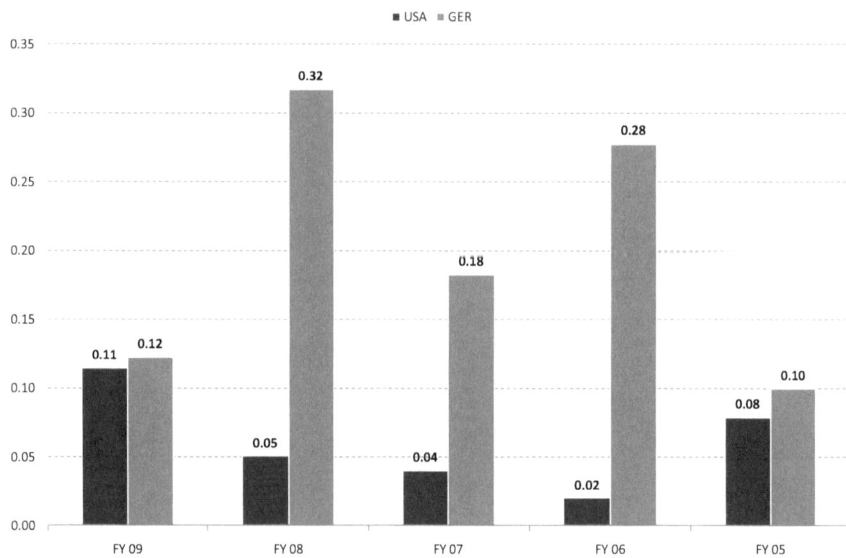

Source: Own Calculations

Once more, the principal component regression provides a much better fit for German institutional investors than it does for US investors. While the average R^2 in the US reaches an exiguous 0.06, Germany reaches a value of 0.20. Looking only at statistically significant R^2 the values change to 0.07 and 0.30 respectively. Comparing the latter values to those of the depreciation PCR, we see little change in the US figure, but more than a bisection of the German figure. Thus, asset allocation is clearly a better predictor of depreciation than investment returns in Germany, whereas it has little explanatory power for either measure in the US. The country patterns observed in

are quasi mirrored. In 2005 and 2009 there is no large difference between the R^2 in both countries whereas from 2006 to 2008 they diverge – in those years the asset allocation of tested German institutional investors had a much larger impact on their performance than in the neighboring years. For the United States, the investment returns of those years were almost completely independent of the implemented asset allocation. A connection between this pattern and the correlation between the invested asset classes can be drawn: A low R^2 indicates a high correlation of the single investments' returns, since returns show a large degree of independence from the asset allocation. Vice versa, a higher R^2 implies a lower correlation between the companies' investments, since in that case, different asset allocations lead to different returns. The conclusion is that the correlation of invested assets in the US increased between 2006 and 2008, whereas the German investors chose assets that had a lower correlation during this period than in the neighboring years. The factors that influence return besides the analyzed asset allocation again are multi-faceted, some of which have been mentioned in the previous chapter.

Figure 16: Principal Component Regression Validation Plots, Investment Returns FY 2008

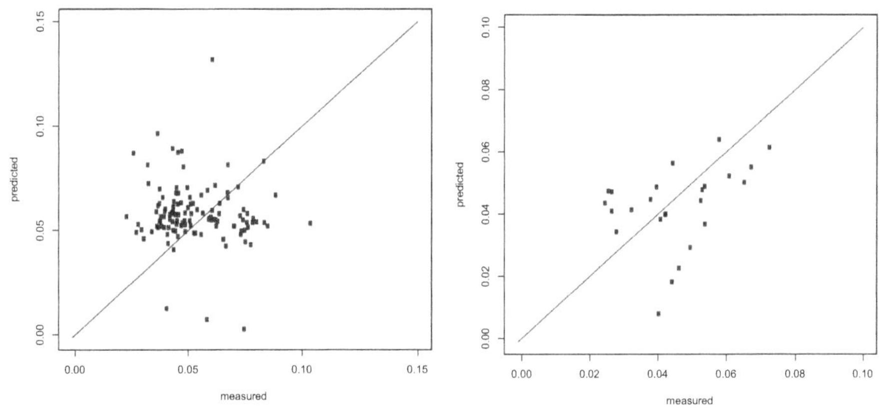

Source: Own Calculations

Figure 16 exemplarily shows the validation plots that picture the measured investment returns to the ones predicted by the principal component regression for the year 2008. 125 observations and forecasts are plotted for the US, compared to 27 for Germany. Not only is the range of measured returns much wider in the US than in Germany, but due to the principal components of the data, the projected values are more scattered as well.

4.4 Conclusions of Empirical Examination

After describing the data and the mathematical approach to the analyses, providing results of the descriptive statistics analysis and analyzing these results by using principal component analysis and regression, this chapter aims at summarizing the outcomes. It gives an overview of the hypotheses that were set up in chapter 3 and shows how the data supports or contradicts them.

Table 2 summarizes the hypotheses and their assessment.

The descriptive statistics analysis provides a meaningful overview of the asset allocation of capital investments between the United States and Germany for both insurance companies and pension funds. The results show similarities between the countries as well as differences in a static picture and in the time series over five years. While returns of insurance companies in both countries show high similarity, the difference to pension funds for professionals in private practice are clearly noticeable. Depreciation is used as a measure of realized risk and shows a massive distinction between insurance companies of the US and Germany. The depreciation quota of German pension funds for professionals in private practice generally ranges in the middle between the insurance companies. Volatility and value at risk are also used as risk measures for market risk of the insurance portfolios. While volatility tends to be slightly higher in the USA, it is the opposite with VaR. Concerning investment return, the average difference between the countries is not very large, while the dynamic picture over time can show interesting distinctions. Standard deviations are also calculated and interpreted for all measures mentioned above.

In order to evaluate the results obtained in the descriptive statistics analyses, principal component regressions are performed to test the effect of asset allocation on depreciation quotas and investment performance. Proposals for the explanation of the low determination coefficients for the United States are given. The analyses show a good fit for the German market. The regressions uncover further differences in investment behavior between the two countries. Potential reasons for differences in asset allocation in addition to the intensively discussed regulation and governance factors are provided.

One question to be answered in this thesis is how regulation and governance impact investment behavior. The calculations to test hypotheses 1 and 2 are shown in Table 1. Across the board, the ranges of investment quotas towards any asset class are larger for the US insurance market than in Germany with the exception of equity investments in 2008. However, as the amount of data for the US is much larger than that of Germany, it is not clear that the wider range stems from differences in regulation only. The standard deviation among companies for any non-equity investment is higher in the United States. However, the data circumstances would play in favor of the contrary development. Hence, it can be inferred that the higher standard deviation is based on different regulation.

Table 1: Differences in Range and Standard Deviation of Asset Allocations for 2005-2009

	EQ 09	FI 09	OA 09	EQ 08	FI 08	OA 08	EQ 07	FI 07	OA 07	EQ 06	FI 06	OA 06	EQ 05	FI 05	OA 05
Range USA-GER	0.46	0.80	0.83	-0.1	0.63	0.86	0.08	0.52	0.77	0.13	0.51	0.77	0.39	0.41	0.77
Stdev USA-GER	0.03	0.12	0.12	-0.1	0.05	0.13	-0.0	0.05	0.11	-0.1	0.01	0.08	-0.1	0.00	0.08

Source: Own Calculations

There is a clear dominance of fixed income investments for insurance companies in the United States, as the average allocation over the observed period amounts to over 80 percent. However, the same measure for consolidated fixed income assets in Germany almost reaches 79 percent. Thus, it cannot be inferred that the prudent person rule in the United States leads to anomalies concerning extreme asset allocations in the insurance industry. In the pension fund industry, the picture is slightly different. While there is no dominant asset class in Germany, equities are clearly preferred by the American investors with an average allocation of 62.5 percent. Whether the increased diversification in this industry in Germany is due to quantitative restrictions cannot be said without dispute; however, pension investors clearly behave differently.

Concerning the subsequently emerging increase in risk as measured by portfolio volatility and daily value at risk, hypothesis 4 cannot be confirmed. While projected portfolio volatility is slightly higher in the US, the corresponding value at risk is marginally lower than in Germany. However, the calculated outcomes do not reflect historical data as experienced by the institutional investors and thus no concluding bottom line can be drawn.

US investors do not reach a significant outperformance over German investors in the time period examined. In fact, the average investment return is slightly lower in the United States. As the PCR indicates, the US return is independent from asset allocation while the German return is not. This fact suggests that the quantitative restrictions on asset allocation in Germany are linked to return. Surprisingly, they do not hinder the German investors in a way that they are outperformed by US investors. However, a curtailing still exists under the assumption that German investors are systematically more successful than American ones.

Another parameter that hints at a beneficial impact of quantitative regulation in Germany is the difference in the depreciation quota between the countries. Hypothesis 6 can be strongly confirmed. With the high determination coefficient that the regression suggests, it appears as if the regulation plays a pivotal role in the origin of this difference. The counterargument that differences in accounting standards might cause the high depreciation quota in the US fades as more and more German companies are using IAS by now compared to 2005 and the effect has not diminished.

Pension funds in the US have a dominant asset class, namely equity, while German pension investors do not exhibit such behavior. This result is in line with the "naïve diversification" bias described by Benartzi and Thaler, who discover a structural overinvestment into the asset class most often provided by company pension plans. With this, hypothesis 7 can be confirmed, assuming the relative number of investment options into equity has not shifted massively since their study.[166]

Hypothesis 14 could not be tested explicitly in this analysis, as sufficient data about the holding period of single investments could not be obtained. An approximation to test the hypothesis, however, can be to look at the pace of change in asset allocation. Here it becomes evident that institutional investors in the insurance industry react in a less pronounced and slower fashion than German insurance investors. The data of interest for this statement lies around the financial crisis of 2008. However, for pension fund investors, the hypothesis is rejected as in this case, US investors show a quicker and more distinct reaction than German investors do.

As the withholding flat tax rate for capital investments has only been implemented in Germany in 2009, it is not possible to test hypothesis 15 yet.

[166] Cf. Benartzi and Thaler (2001), Table 9

Table 2: Overview and Assessment of Hypotheses

H1: Broader allocation range within asset classes in the US	Higher absolute range for every class and year in the US.[167] Lower average range for both insurance companies and pension funds in the time series.
H2: Higher variance of allocation in the US	True for fixed income and other assets
H3: Dominance of asset classes in the US	Dominance of fixed income for insurances, but no significant difference to Germany. Dominance of equity in US pensions.
H4: Increased portfolio volatility and higher VaR in the US	Slightly higher volatility in the US and slightly lower VaR in the US
H5: Superior performance in US	Slightly lower return before taxes
H6: Reduced portfolio risk in Germany	Average depreciation quota much lower than in the US
H7: Naïve diversification of US pension assets	Higher equity proportion in US pension assets in line with Benartzi and Thaler[168]
H8: Increased home bias of insurance investments	Not essential to test in the setting of this thesis
H9: No expenditure difference due to compliance efforts	Not essential to test in the setting of this thesis
H10: Skewed investment performance in Germany	Not explicitly tested, yet no conclusive evidence can be found in raw data
H11: Impact of expense structure on investment behavior	Not essential to test in the setting of this thesis
H12: Impact of tax regime on investment behavior	Not essential to test in the setting of this thesis
H13: Tendency for US pension investors to invest at home	High percentage invested at home according to EBRI studies[169]
H14: US investors show a tendency for long-term investments	Not explicitly tested, but sluggish changes in asset allocation link to proof
H15: German investors enhance their holding period after 2009	Data basis is not resilient concerning its duration yet
H16: Outperformance of pension funds with strong governance	Not essential to test in the setting of this thesis

167 Exception: Equity allocation in 2008
168 Cf. Benartzi and Thaler (2001)
169 Cf. EBRI 2006-2010

5. Implications of Findings

Up to this point, this thesis has shown the scientific approach of asset management and the implementation in real life as well as the differences in regulation and corporate governance for insurance companies and pension funds between the United States and Germany. In addition, data from a time period of five years was used to compare the investment behavior of institutional investors in both countries and analyze the impact that regulation and governance of the respective country have on asset allocation, several measures of portfolio risk and investment return. From the conclusions and links drawn so far, it is possible to derive practical implications for both regulators and institutional asset managers.

5.1 Implications for Regulators

Regulators in the United States and Germany follow two different regimes regarding the regulation of asset allocation for institutional investors. While US regulators largely rely on the prudent person rule and provide big margins for action to asset managers, the German BaFin imposes strict quantitative limits on the allocation for insurance and pension funds. The results of the study conducted in the course of this thesis show that the supposedly restrictive policy in Germany is in fact very powerful. While it does not inhibit investment performance in comparison to US asset managers, it strongly reduces realized risk measured by depreciation. A measure mentioned earlier, to put performance into relation to the risk taken, is the Sharpe ratio. When taking the 10 year US T-Note interest rate as an approximation of the risk-free rate, German investors reach a higher projected Sharpe ratio of 29.51% compared to 21.62% attained by their US equivalents. In addition, the allegedly tight asset allocation corset in Germany still leaves investors enough room to adjust to changes in the investment environment quickly. Immediate and considerable shifts in asset allocation can be observed during the financial crisis. It can be stated that the quantitative restrictions in Germany are more efficient than the prudent person rule implemented in the United States and should therefore be considered for adoption by US regulators.

Compliance is another regulation that is set up in a stricter way in Germany than it is in the US. It is useful for both market participants and regulators. However, the line between additional effort associated with compliance requirements for the investment firm and the marginal benefit of the additional regulation compliance is thin. The additional expenditures are likely to be passed on to consumers through increased fees. Future research could lead to finding an optimal liaison between the antagonists, which can then be transferred to a more efficient regulation.

Disclosure requirements have assimilated between the countries over the last years. Through implementation of the European Commission suggestion that German companies file reports in accordance with IAS, German disclosures are expected to be more detailed than they were before and close the gap to US reports. Currently, the only unsatisfying condition in disclosure regulation is the enforcement of the EC regulation, which still leaves room for institutional investors, especially the smaller ones, to provide favorable information to the public only. German regulators could close this loophole and level the playing field for all institutional investors.

As the institutional investment market is polypolistic, there is no immediate need to regulate it in terms of setting a limit to expenses charged to consumers. The US insurance market shows no signs of critical market power for a small number of institutional investors, whereas the German market is characterized by the sway of a couple of big players. Based on assets under management, the Herfindahl-Hirschman-Index for the US shows a value of 0.11 compared to 0.27 in Germany. German regulators should keep an eye on this development and step in when necessary in order to keep competition at an adequate level and expenses for consumers within their natural range of the competitive market.

Concerning taxes, the schemes between the United States and Germany have assimilated as well. This is especially important in a globalized world with little barriers for capital investments and companies open to relocation. The US regulators place emphasis on enhancing the home bias through incentivizing local investments. The effectiveness and reasonability of this measure was not specifically examined in this thesis, but an eye-catching advantage of this policy could not be observed in measures of return or risk. Future studies can elucidate this research gap. Both the US and Germany exhibit a high diversity of tax jurisdiction due to parts of the regulation being imposed on either state or even local level. This can distort the competitiveness of companies in the industry and have vast effects on the local economies. The potential magnitude of such effects should be kept in mind by regulators.

5.2 Implications for Institutional Investors

While institutional investors are generally faced with the regulation that is forced upon them, corporate governance consists of self-imposed measures, that to a large extent use the best practice as a role model, and has no direct juridical consequences if neglected.

The use of efficient corporate governance, however, can lead to better investment management as shown by Clark and Urwin who provide a link between good governance and strong fund performance in their study of pension funds.[170] It has not yet been studied whether this result can be extrapolated to other industries, such as the insurance industry.

There is no immediate reason why the companies in the United States should follow a different corporate governance practice from the ones in Germany. Thus, the standards proposed by international organizations such as the OECD or IAIS are universally applicable. The suggestions and best practices mentioned in chapter 3.2 are developed by such organizations in cooperation with practitioners and therefore provide a good guideline for both countries evaluated in this study. However, a one to one transfer does not seem adequate, as company characteristics or the current company situation might demand different needs than suggested in the general setting of the best practice guidelines. Since there has been no recent study as to what extent the best practice suggestions have been implemented in either country, it is delicate to draw conclusions for improvements of institutional investors' behavior in this paper.

As investors in Germany are faced with stricter rules concerning asset allocation than American investors are, but at the same time experience a better risk-reward ratio than the latter, it appears expedient for the latter to study the investment behavior of the former. Through the prudent person rules, US investors are generally able to invest in the same assets as German investors do and thus achieve similar investment results. Especially when looking at the high depreciation quota US investors have faced over the time period of this study compared to their German equivalents, they should adapt the strategies used by the latter and adjust them to fulfill the specific needs of their country and client base.

6. Conclusion

This chapter summarizes the content of this study concisely and provides an overview of future research potential in this field of finance and asset management.

6.1 Summary

The aim of the thesis at hand was to evaluate the impact of regulation and governance on investment behavior of institutional investors and to reveal differences and similarities

170 Cf. Clark and Urwin (2007)

between the United States and Germany caused by the former, based on an empirical analysis and insights from industry experts.

The first part of this study presents the theory surrounding institutional asset management and the current state of the literature in the field. The scientific approach to investment management, an industry analysis and an overview over recent developments provide principles of institutional asset management. The theoretical part of this study furthermore compares the current state of regulation for institutional investors between the United States and Germany and shows best practices for corporate governance for insurance companies and pension funds. The largest differences between the countries can be found in the investment regulation. While the US regulators rely on prudent person rules or fairly lax asset allocation quotas for insurances, the German market is highly regulated through a multitude of quantitative restrictions on investments and asset allocation. Pension funds in Germany have to follow the same strict guidelines, whereas pensions in the United States are managed on an individual level and are not significantly regulated. The opposite is true for disclosure regulation: While US companies have to comply with detailed IAS directives, German investors can choose to value their investments following the HGB or IAS. Non-public companies do not have to provide investment information, which could lead to a bias in public data.

Sixteen hypotheses are derived from differences in regulation and governance. These hypotheses are discussed with both regulators and asset managers in the practical part of the thesis. The empirical examination of the data includes statistical analyses to show differences and similarities between the investment behavior of institutional investors of the United States and Germany. The differences are further analyzed to determine the significance of regulation for the statistical differences. Principal component regressions show that a large share of the depreciation quota and investment return can be explained through asset allocation in Germany whereas this relationship does not hold for the US. It can be concluded that the quantitative regulation in Germany is efficient since it does not put investors to a disadvantage concerning performance compared to their American peers, yet provides a much more secure risk management in terms of depreciation.

Implications for both regulators and investors are drawn from the analyses' results. On basis of the better relationship between risk and return of German investors and the proven connection between quantitative regulation in Germany and investment results, it appears reasonable for US regulators to adopt German standards. However, it is not clear whether a similar regulation would lead to the same results in the United States, as many other factors enter the equation for the relationship between risk and return. The assimilation in other fields of regulation should be encouraged by regulators to create a level playing field in the global world of asset management. This refers especially to disclosure and taxation issues that can differ greatly, even within countries or regions. The corporate governance best practices should be adopted and adapted by institutional investors in both countries for two major reasons. Firstly, the positive relationship between investment return and a good corporate governance practice has been proven in several studies and secondly, a strong corporate and investment governance code defines clear processes that can be beneficial in many ways, e.g. through the reduction of corruption issues.

6.2 OUTLOOK

From the academic perspective, this thesis revealed a number of research opportunities. While the field for mutual funds and pension funds has been the subject of many studies, research on insurance capital management is still at a very early development stage. In addition, the German regulatory environment in connection to asset management is almost untouched. A few hypotheses derived in the course of this paper could not be tested in the setting of this thesis, but are expected to offer interesting insights into the asset management industry.

The efficiency of single quantitative restrictions has not been studied yet, but could provide the industry with useful knowledge for meaningful and accurate limits. For such a study, a comparison between the actual needs and requests of investors can be compared to the current regulatory corset they face. This includes the extent to which the home bias of investors is increased through regulatory requirements. The goal of this study would be to match the requirements of the regulators with the needs of investors in a more efficient way than it is currently done.

The impact of some decisive factors for investment behavior that this thesis touched upon can be measured in order to find the driving forces behind investment behavior, especially in the US. Such factors include the expense structure as well as the tax regime that investors are confronted with.

The tendency for long-term investments of US investors remains untested in this study. A long-term study can reveal the benefits and downsides of this regulatory action and point at possible implications for regulators in other countries. As German investors are facing a similar situation since legislation changed in 2009, the results can be compared to receive a more tenable picture.

Since an outperformance is reached by pension funds with strong corporate governance, it suggests itself to test similar effects for the insurance industry. Due to its qualitative character, the implementation of corporate governance standards has not been tested empirically or compared in either of the countries studied in this paper. The implications that a strong governance code can have not only on performance, but also on risk and other investment behavior are essential to understand in the light of the financial crisis and help answer the question whether corporate governance should be regulated in a similar fashion as capital investments.

Appendix

Appendix 1: Summary of Statistical Analyses

	FY 09					FY 08					FY 07				
	USA Ins	401(k)	GER Total	Ins	VW	USA Ins	401(k)	GER Total	Ins	VW	USA Ins	401(k)	GER Total	Ins	VW
Average Allocation to Equity	3.61%	58.50%	8.78%	7.71%	40.59%	3.62%	54.50%	10.82%	9.23%	39.37%	4.76%	66.50%	19.22%	18.73%	39.59%
Average Allocation to Fixed Income	84.87%	37.50%	87.80%	88.97%	53.17%	82.19%	41.50%	84.42%	86.19%	52.72%	75.45%	30.50%	68.70%	69.20%	47.36%
Average Allocation to Other	11.52%	4.00%	3.41%	3.32%	6.24%	14.19%	4.00%	4.76%	4.58%	7.91%	19.79%	3.00%	12.09%	12.06%	13.05%
Average Return	4.66%		5.30%	5.30%	5.30%	5.88%		4.30%	4.99%	3.75%	5.44%		5.52%	5.30%	5.76%
Standard Deviation of Returns	1.77%		2.21%	2.39%	2.11%	6.28%		1.93%	2.59%	0.94%	2.22%		1.34%	1.56%	1.05%
Average Depreciation Quota	0.81%		0.22%	0.05%	0.46%	1.01%		0.90%	0.02%	1.60%	0.87%		0.11%	0.03%	0.20%
Standard Deviation of Depreciation	1.35%		0.30%	0.08%	0.33%	1.87%		1.73%	0.03%	2.09%	1.58%		0.18%	0.03%	0.23%
Average Portfolio Volatility	4.66%			2.98%		5.57%			5.68%		3.34%			3.13%	
Standard Deviation of Volatility	1.86%			0.95%		1.22%			3.79%		0.55%			1.51%	
Average Portfolio VaR (99%)	0.64%			0.41%		0.89%			1.15%		0.59%			0.44%	
Standard Deviation of VaR	0.27%			0.13%		0.30%			0.64%		0.13%			0.21%	
Sharpe Ratio	0.28			0.66		0.38			0.22		0.21			0.18	
Number of Companies	124		19	11	8	125		27	12	15	138		25	13	12
Funds included in mm USD	2,048,912	1,210,414	996,140	951,473	44,667	1,913,637	1,092,468	942,930	871,560	71,370	2,348,043	1,425,142	1,283,805	1,243,342	40,463
Percentage of Market included		44.00%		64.07%			47.00%		59.33%			47.00%		87.03%	
Market Size		2,750,941		1,554,853			2,324,400		1,589,177			3,032,217		1,475,055	
Herfindahl-Hirschman-Index	0.09		0.25	0.25		0.10		0.22	0.22		0.12		0.31	0.31	
Average Exchange Rate					1.3946					1.4721					1.3704
Performance of Risk-Free Rate	3.33%	3.33%	3.33%	3.33%	3.33%	3.76%	3.76%	3.76%	3.76%	3.76%	4.75%	4.75%	4.75%	4.75%	4.75%
Return R^2	0.11		0.12			0.05		0.32			0.04		0.18		
Return p-Value	0.00		0.35			0.04		0.01			0.06		0.11		
Depreciation R^2	0.00		0.32			0.08		0.23			0.01		0.24		
Depreciation p-Value	0.77		0.12			0.01		0.18			0.55		0.20		

Statistically Significant at 5% Level
Statistically Significant at 10% Level

	FY 06					FY 05					Average				
	USA Ins	401(k)	GER Total	Ins	VW	USA Ins	401(k)	GER Total	Ins	VW	USA Ins	401(k)	GER Total	Ins	VW
Average Allocation to Equity	5.28%	66.50%	17.25%	16.69%	41.94%	4.74%	66.50%	18.52%	18.36%	59.68%	4.40%	62.50%	14.92%	14.15%	44.23%
Average Allocation to Fixed Income	79.50%	30.50%	73.47%	74.11%	45.13%	79.85%	32.50%	74.93%	75.10%	31.36%	80.37%	34.50%	77.86%	78.71%	45.95%
Average Allocation to Other	15.22%	3.00%	9.29%	9.21%	12.93%	15.41%	1.00%	6.55%	6.54%	8.96%	15.23%	3.00%	7.22%	7.14%	9.82%
Average Return	5.19%		5.31%	5.43%	5.12%	4.67%		4.77%	5.23%	3.04%	5.16%		5.04%	5.25%	4.59%
Standard Deviation of Returns	1.89%		1.71%	2.11%	0.78%	1.77%		2.01%	1.47%	2.96%	2.78%		1.84%	2.02%	1.57%
Average Depreciation Quota	0.95%		0.06%	0.04%	0.10%	0.79%		0.10%	0.03%	0.34%	0.89%		0.28%	0.03%	0.54%
Standard Deviation of Depreciation	1.95%		0.08%	0.04%	0.12%	1.24%		0.30%	0.05%	0.66%	1.60%		0.52%	0.05%	0.69%
Average Portfolio Volatility	2.54%			3.51%		2.63%			3.03%		3.75%			3.67%	
Standard Deviation of Volatility	0.34%			1.56%		0.73%			1.53%		0.94%			1.87%	
Average Portfolio VaR (99%)	0.38%			0.60%		0.44%			0.51%		0.59%			0.62%	
Standard Deviation of VaR	0.09%			0.25%		0.12%			0.25%		0.18%			0.30%	
Sharpe Ratio	0.10			0.14		0.11			0.28		21.62%			29.51%	
Number of Companies	146		26	16	10	151		24	19	5	137		24	14	10
Funds included in mm USD	2,256,563	1,228,033	1,206,741	1,173,357	33,384	2,051,048	1,000,000	1,077,227	1,072,037	5,190	2,123,641	1,191,211	1,101,369	1,062,354	39,015
Percentage of Market included		46.00%		93.93%			42.00%		74.92%			45.20%		75.86%	
Market Size		2,669,637		1,284,772			2,380,952		1,437,887						
Herfindahl-Hirschman-Index	0.12		0.27	0.27		0.10		0.28	0.28		0.11		0.27	0.27	
Average Exchange Rate					1.2562					1.2442					
Performance of Risk-Free Rate	4.93%	4.93%	4.93%	4.93%	4.93%	4.38%	4.38%	4.38%	4.38%	4.38%					
Return R²	0.02		0.28			0.08		0.10			0.07		0.30		
Return p-Value	0.24		0.02			0.00		0.37							
Depreciation R²	0.03		0.64			0.02		0.70			0.08		0.67		
Depreciation p-Value	0.12		0.00			0.32		0.00							

Statistically Significant at 5% Level
Statistically Significant at 10% Level

Appendix 2: PCR Validation Plots, Depreciation and Return GER 2005

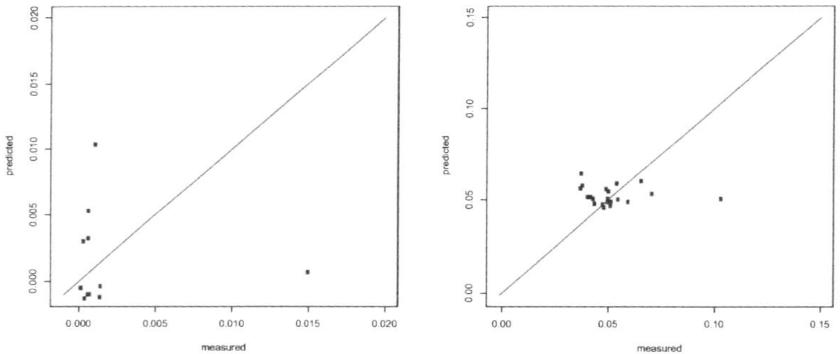

Appendix 4: PCR Validation Plots, Depreciation and Return GER 2007

XIII

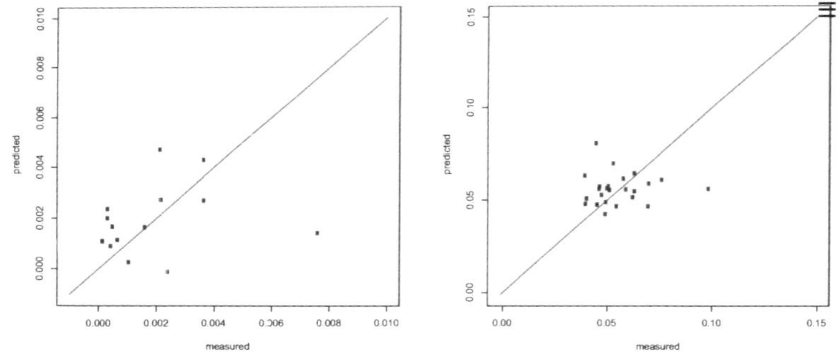

Appendix 3: PCR Validation Plots, Depreciation and Return GER 2006

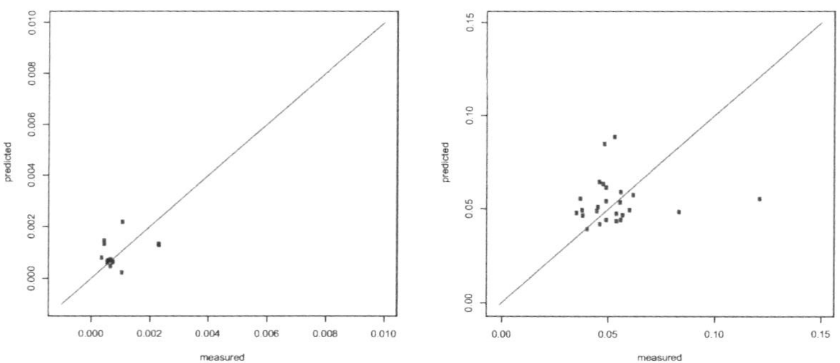

Appendix 5: PCR Validation Plots, Depreciation and Return GER 2008

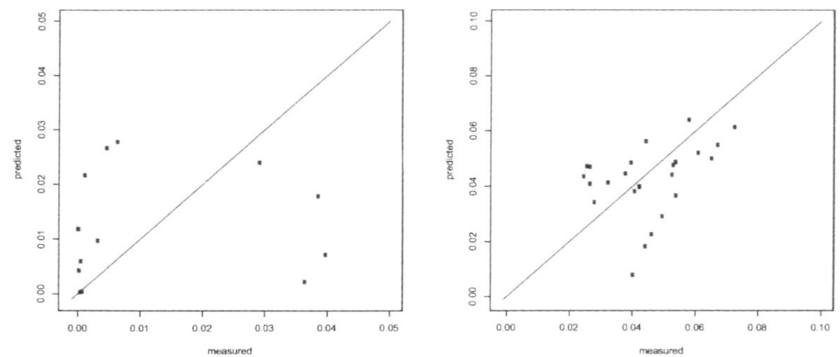

Appendix 6: PCR Validation Plots, Depreciation and Return GER 2009

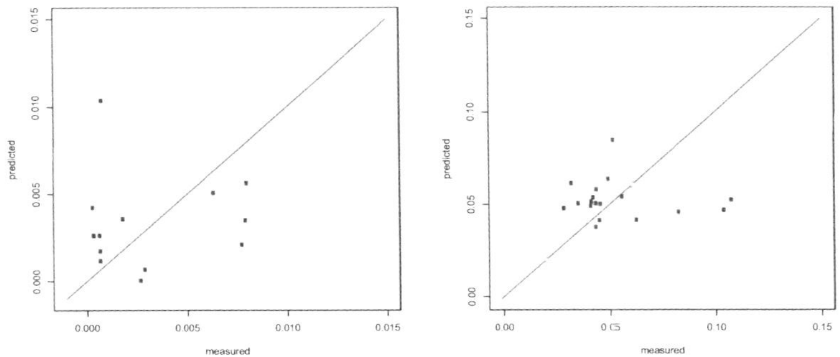

Appendix 7: PCR Validation Plots, Depreciation and Return USA 2005

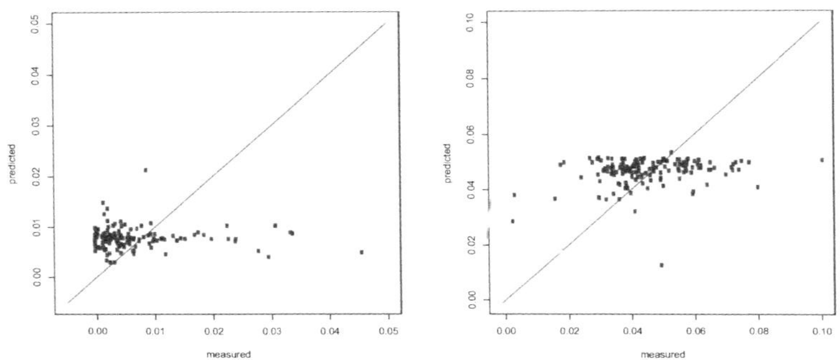

Appendix 8: PCR Validation Plots, Depreciation and Return USA 2006

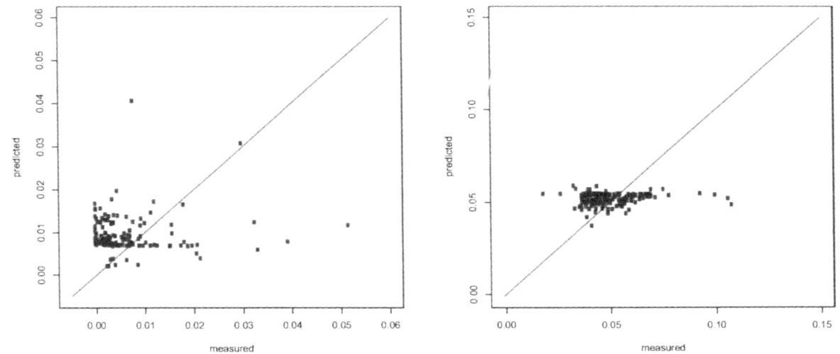

Appendix 9: PCR Validation Plots, Depreciation and Return USA 2007

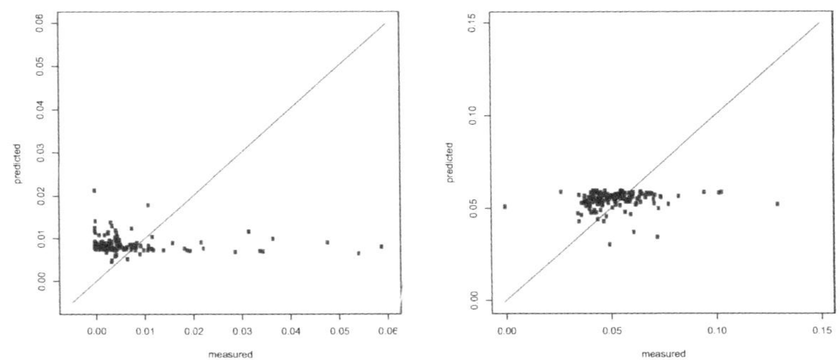

Appendix 10: PCR Validation Plots, Depreciation and Return USA 2008

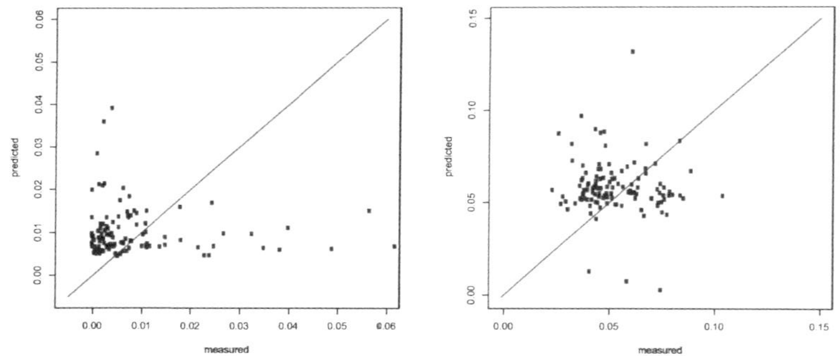

Appendix 11: PCR Validation Plots, Depreciation and Return USA 2009

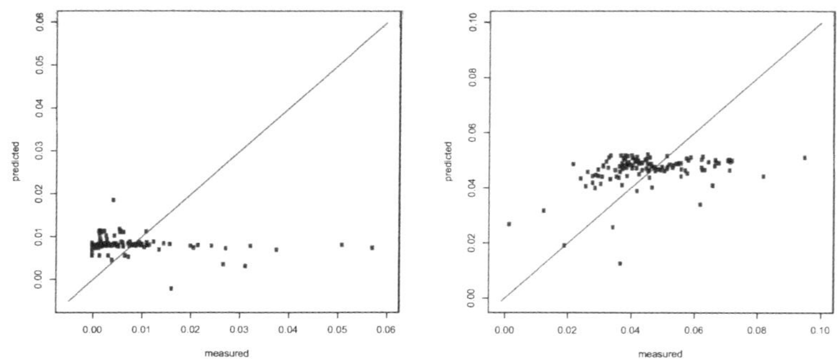

Appendix 12: Questionnaire for Pension Funds for Professionals in Private Practice

1. Do you experience the regulation of asset allocation of pension funds for professionals in private practice through quantitative limits as interference in the investment process?

2. Do you see advantages for your organization through the quantitative restrictions for investments and asset allocation?

3. Do disadvantages develop from your regulation – also in comparison to US pension funds that follow the prudent person rule and do not have to comply with strict investment and asset allocation quotas?

4. Is the compliance with investment regulation for pension funds for professionals in private practice associated with additional work and expenses for your organization? If so, do the positive effects of the regulation compensate this at the least?

5. My study shows a very similar investment performance of German institutional investors compared to their American equivalents while a much lower depreciation quota is obtained in Germany. Would you trace this finding back to the quantitative regulation or rather to other structural differences between the countries?

6. What roles does corporate governance play in your organization's investment process?

7. How present is acting according to corporate governance best practices among institutional investors in Germany – also in comparison to the USA?

List of References

Abdallah, M., Karolia, E., Ong, J., & Owens, K. (2009). Shariah-Compliant Funds: A Whole New World of Investment.

Abdi, S., Stanley, M., Rana, N., Mitchell, R., Taher, A., Abboud, R., et al. (2008). The Islamic Funds & Investments Report 2008 - Outlining Opportunities in the Asset Management Landscape.

Adams, M. (1995). Return on Investment Assets and the Organisational Characteristics of the Life Insurance Firm: New Zealand Evidence. School of Applied and International Economics, Massey University.

Agnew, J., & Szykman, L. (2005). Asset Allocation and Information Overload: The Influence of Information Display, Asset Choice, and Investor Experience. Journal of Behavioral Finance, 6(2), 57-70.

Ambachtsheer, K., Capelle, R., & Scheibelhut, T. (1998). Improving Pension Fund Performance. Financial Analysts Journal, 54, 15-21.

Ang, A., & Bekaert, G. (2002). International Asset Allocation with Regime Shifts. Review of Financial Studies, 15(4), 1137-1187.

BaFin (2005). Rundschreiben 15/2005 (VA) (Anlage des gebundenen Vermögens; Anlagemanagement und interne Kontrollverfahren). Bonn/Frankfurt: Bundesanstalt für Finanzdienstleistungsaufsicht.

BaFin (2009). Rundschreiben 3/2009 (VA) - Aufsichtsrechtliche Mindestanforderungen an das Risikomanagement (MaRisk VA). Bonn/Frankfurt: Bundesanstalt für Finanzdienstleistungsaufsicht.

BaFin (2010a). Entwurf eines Rundschreibens. Bonn/Frankfurt: Bundesanstalt für Finanzdienstleistungsaufsicht.

BaFin (2010b). Jahresbericht 2009. Bonn/Frankfurt: Bundesanstalt für Finanzdienstleistungsaufsicht..

Balding, C. (2008). A Portfolio Analysis of Sovereign Wealth Funds. Irvine.

Barbary, V., & Chin, E. (2009). Testing Time - Sovereign Wealth Funds in the Middle East & North Africa and the Global Financial Crisis.

Barberis, N., & Shleifer, A. (2003). Style Investing. Journal of Financial Economics, 68(2), 161-199.

Benartzi, S., & Thaler, R. H. (2001). Naive Diversification Strategies in Defined Contribution Saving Plans. American Economic Review, 91(1), 79–98.

Blake, D., Lehmann, B. N., & Timmermann, A. (1999). Asset Allocation Dynamics and Pension Fund Performance. The Journal of Business, 72(4), 429-461.

Brennan, M. J., Schwartz, E. S., & Lagnado, R. (1997). Strategic Asset Allocation. Journal of Economic Dynamics and Control, 21(8-9), 1377-1403.

Brown, K. C., & Van Harlow, W. (2002). Staying the Course: The Impact of Investment Style Consistency on Mutual Fund Performance. Austin, TX.

Brown, S., & Goetzmann, W. (1995). Performance persistence. Journal of Finance, 50(2), 679–698.

Brown, S., & Goetzmann, W. (1997). Mutual Fund Styles. Journal of Financial Economics, 43(3), 373-399.

Canner, N., Mankiw, N. G., & Weil, D. N. (1997). An Asset Allocation Puzzle. The American Economic Review, 87(1), 181–191.

Carhart, M. M. (1997). On Persistence in Mutual Fund Performance. Journal of Finance, 52(1), 57–82.

Chan, L. K. C., Chen, H. L., & Lakonishok, J. (2002). On Mutual Fund Investment Styles. Review of Financial Studies, 15(5), 1407-1437.

Chan, L. K. C., Karceski, J., & Lakonishok, J. (1998). The Risk and Return from Factors. Journal of Financial and Quantitative Analysis, 33(2), 159–188.

Choi, J. J., Laibson, D., Madrian, B. C., & Metrick, A. (2002). Defined Contribution Pensions: Plan Rules, Participant Choices, and the Path of Least Resistance. Tax Policy and the Economy, 16(1), 67–113.

Clark, G. L., & Urwin, R. (2007). Best-Practice Investment Management: Lessons for Asset Owners from the Oxford–Watson Wyatt Project on Governance. Oxford.

Coggin, T. D., Fabozzi, F. J., & Rahman, S. (1993). The Investment Performance of US Equity Pension Fund Managers: An Empirical Investigation. Journal of Finance, 48(3), 1039–1055.

Davis, E. P. (2000). Portfolio Regulation of Life Insurance Companies and Pension Funds. London.

Davis, E. P. (2002a). The European Pension Management Industry. London.

Davis, E. P. (2002b). Pension Fund Management and International Investment - A Global Perspective (pp. 7-15). London: Pensions Institute.

Davis, E. P. (2002c). Prudent Person Rules or Quantitative Restrictions? The Regulation of Long-Term Institutional Investors' Portfolios. Journal of Pension Economics and Finance, 1(02), 1-32.

Davis, J. L. (1994). The Cross-Section of Realized Stock Returns: The Pre-COMPUSTAT Evidence. Journal of Finance, 49(5), 1579-1593.

Davis, J. L. (2001). Mutual Fund Performance and Manager Style. Financial Analysts Journal, 57(1), 19-27.

Del Guercio, D., & Hawkins, J. (1999). The Motivation and Impact of Pension Fund Activism. Journal of Financial Economics, 52(3), 293-340.

Dickinson, G. (1998). Issues in the Effective Regulation of the Asset Allocation of Life Insurance Companies. In H. Blommestein & N. Funke (Eds.), Institutional Investors in the new Financial Landscape. Paris: OECD.

Doyle, R. J. (2003). Allocation of Expenses in a Defined Contribution Plan.

Elton, E. J., Gruber, M. J., & Blake, C. R. (1996). The Persistence of Risk-Adjusted Mutual Fund Performance. Journal of Business, 69(2), 133–157.

Employee Retirement Income Security Act of 1974 (ERISA) (1974). Washington.

English, T. F., Stading, D. R., Roth, S. E., & Krus, C. M. (2005). Corporate Governance Best Practices For Insurance Companies: The Current Perspective.

Ernst & Young (2008). IFRS 7 in the Insurance Industry.

Eurosif (2006). European SRI Study 2006.

Faff, R. W. (2003). Creating Fama and French Factors with Style. The Financial Review, 38(2), 311–322.

Fama, E. F., & French, K. R. (1992). The Cross-Section of Expected Stock Returns. Journal of Finance, 47(2), 427–465.

Fama, E. F., & French, K. R. (1993). Common Risk Factors in the Returns on Stocks and Bonds. Journal of Financial Economics, 33(1), 3–56.

Fama, E. F., & French, K. R. (1996). Multifactor Explanations of Asset Pricing Anomalies. Journal of Finance, 51(1), 55–84.

Figeac, A. (2007). Socially Responsible Investment und Umweltorientiertes Venture Capital. Berlin.

Fotak, V., Bortolotti, B., Megginson, W., & Miracky, W. (2008). The Financial Impact of Sovereign Wealth Fund Investments in Listed Companies. Norman, OK and Turin, Italy.

Franks, J., & Mayer, C. (2001). Risks and Regulation in European Asset Management: Is There a Role for Capital Requirements. Oxford.

Frantz, C., Chenut, X., & Walhin, J. (2003). Pricing and Capital Allocation for Unit-Linked Life Insurance Contracts with Minimum Death Guarantee. Proceedings of the AFIR Colloquium, Maastricht (pp. 1-17).

French, K. R., & Poterba, J. M. (1991). Investor Diversification and International Equity Markets. American Economic Review, 81(2), 222-226.

Gait, A. H., & Worthington, A. C. (2009). A Primer on Islamic Finance: Definitions, Sources, Principles and Methods. Nathan, Australia.

Garvey, J., Flanagan, J., Foy, J., Everson, M., Meltzer, G., & McDonnell, P. (2010). The New Rule of 10% - The Coming Pension Crisis, Higher Savings Rates, and Fundamental Changes in the US Financial Services Industry.

Gesetz über die Beaufsichtigung der Versicherungsunternehmen (Versicherungsaufsichtsgesetz - VAG) (2010). Berlin: Deutscher Bundestag.

Gesetz über die Beaufsichtigung der Versicherungsunternehmen und der Versorgungswerke der Freien Berufe im Land Nordrhein-Westfalen (Landesversicherungsaufsichtsgesetz - VAG NRW) (1999). Landtag Nordrhein-Westfalen.

Goldman, R. (2000). The Development of the "Prudent Man" Concept in Relation to Pension Schemes. Pensions, an International Journal, 5, 219-224.

Grinblatt, M., & Titman, S. (1992). The Persistence of Mutual Fund Performance. Journal of Finance, 47(5), 1977–1984.

Grinold, R. C. (1993). Is Beta Dead Again?. Financial Analysts Journal, 49(4), 28–34.

Gruber, M. J. (1996). Another Puzzle: The Growth in Actively Managed Mutual Funds. Journal of finance, 51(3), 783–810.

Göttsche, M. (2007). Neue Unternehmenssteuer: Die Änderungen. Versicherungen News. Retrieved December 20, 2010, from http://www.versicherungen-blog.net/2007/03/14/neue-unternehmenssteuer-die-aenderungen/.

Handelsgesetzbuch (HGB) (2010). Berlin: Deutscher Bundestag.

Harlow, W. V. (1991). Asset Allocation in a Downside-Risk Framework. Financial Analysts Journal, 47(5), 28–40.

Haugen, R. A., & Lakonishok, J. (1988). The Incredible January Effect. Homewood: Dow Jones Irwin.

Haughton, K., & Christopherson, J. (1989). Equity Style Indexes: Tools for Better Performance Evaluation and Plan Management. Tacoma.

He, J., & Ng, L. K. (1994). Economic Forces, Fundamental Variables, and Equity Returns. Journal of Business, 67(4), 599–609.

Hoyos-Gomez, A., Huber, M., & Schachner, M. (2008). Controlling Costs in European Asset Management. McKinsey Quarterly, (February).

Hwang, S., & Satchell, S. E. (2007). The Disappearance of Style in the US Equity Market. Applied Financial Economics, 17(8), 597–613.

IAIS (2003). The Insurance Core Principles on Corporate Governance. Basel.

IAIS & OECD (2009). Issues Paper on Corporate Governance.

IGG (2010). Looking After Your DC Plan - A Good Practice Guide for Employers. Business Voice, (November 2010).

Internal Revenue Code of 1986. (1986).

IASB (2010). International Financial Reporting Standard 7.

Investment Company Institute (2010). 2010 Investment Company Fact Book. Washington.

Investment Management Association (2010). Asset Management in the UK 2009-2010 - The IMA Annual Survey. Management. London.

Jackson, P. L. (2007). ERISA Compliance. Smart Business Magazine, (February).

Jansson, S. (1983). The Fine Art of Window Dressing. Institutional Investor, 139-140.

Johnson, S. (2007). The Rise of Sovereign Wealth Funds. Finance and Development, 44(3), 56-59.

Jorion, P. (2001). Value at Risk: The New Benchmark for Managing Financial Risk. McGraw-Hill.

Judd, C., & Yin, L. (2010). 2010 Global Pension Asset Study. London.

Kahneman, D., & Tversky, A. (1974). Judgment Under Uncertainty: Heuristics and Biases. Science, 185(4157), 1124-1131.

Keim, D. B., & Madhavan, A. (1997). Transactions Costs and Investment Style: An Inter-Exchange Analysis of Institutional Equity Trades. Journal of Financial Economics, 46(3), 265–292.

Kirton, R. J., & Haynes, A. T. (1953). The Structure of a Life Office. Transactions of the Faculty of Actuaries, 21.

Kramer, K., Beardsley, B., Kumar, M., Maguire, A., Morel, P., Tang, T., et al. (2010). Global Asset Management 2010 - In Search of Stable Growth. Boston.

Lakonishok, J., Shleifer, A., Thaler, R., & Vishny, R. (1991). Window Dressing by Pension Fund Managers. The American Economic Review, 81(2), 227–231.

Lannoo, K., & Levin, M. (2003). Pan-European Asset Management - Achievements and Regulatory Impediments. Brussels.

Markowitz, H. (1952). Portfolio Selection. Journal of Finance, 7, 77-91.

Maslakovic, M. (2010). Fund Management 2010. London.

Merton, R. C. (1969). Lifetime Portfolio Selection under Uncertainty: The Continuous-Time Case. The Review of Economics and Statistics, 51(3), 247–257.

Mevik, B. H., & Wehrens, R. (2007). The pls Package: Principal Component and Partial Least Squares Regression in R. Journal of Statistical Software, 18(2), 1–24.

Möhring, H.-J. (2010). Feri-Umfrage: Profianleger sind optimistisch - aber mutlos. Financial Times Deutschland. Retrieved January 26, 2011, from http://www.ftd.de/finanzen/maerkte/anleihen-devisen/:feri-umfrage-profianleger-sind-optimistisch-aber-mutlos/50209380.html.

OECD (2000). Issues Paper on Investment Regulation. Paris.

OECD (2003). Survey of Investment Regulation of Pension Funds. Paris.

Payne, J. (1996). When Time Is Money: Decision Behavior under Opportunity-Cost Time Pressure. Organizational Behavior and Human Decision Processes, 66(2), 131-152.

Penman, W. (1933). A Review of Investment Principles and Practices. The Journal, 64, 121-152.

Poweleit, M. (2009). map-report Nr. 719-720: Lebensversicherungs-Rating: p-rating. Artlenburg.

Prabhakar, R. (2009). And Then There was One: Conglomeration, Internationalization, and the Formation of Consolidated Financial Supervisors.

Quigley, G., & Sinquefield, R. A. (2000). Performance of UK Equity Unit Trusts. Journal of Asset Management, 1(1), 72–92.

R Development Core Team (2008). R: A Language and Environment for Statistical Computing. (R Development Core Team, Eds.). Vienna: R Foundation for Statistical Computing.

Randall, S. (1999). Insurance Regulation in the United States: Regulatory Federalism and the National Association of Insurance Commissioners. Florida State University Law Review, 26(625), 625–1177.

Rolt, C., Young, J., & Lofts, G. (2009). Cost Management in a More Regulated Asset Management Industry.

Rouwenhorst, K. G. (2004). The Origins of Mutual Funds. New Haven.

Saluzzi, M., & Hage, K. (2010). Insights & Views from PriceWaterhouseCoopers' Global Asset Management Practice. Asset Management News, (March).

Samuelson, P. A. (1969). Lifetime Portfolio Selection by Dynamic Stochastic Programming. The Review of Economics and Statistics, 51(3), 239–246.

Schanz, D. (2009). International Tax Strategy. Vallendar.

Schäfer, H. (2001). Triple Bottom Line Investing–Ethik, Rendite und Risiko in der Kapitalanlage. Zeitschrift für das gesamte Kreditwesen, 54(13), 740–744.

Seymour, D., Brown, T., Pettifer, R., & Suglia, J. J. (2010). Keeping Ahead of the Curve: Investment Management in the New Regulatory Landscape.

Sharpe, W. F. (1966). Mutual Fund Performance. Journal of Business, 39(1), 119–138.

Sharpe, W. F. (1992). Asset Allocation: Management Style and Performance Measurement. Journal of Portfolio Management, 18(2), 7-19.

Shuster, A. (2009). International Comparison of Insurance Taxation. New York City.

Sionna Investment Managers (2010). Sionna's Relative Value Investing Style. Retrieved November 2010, from http://www.sionna.ca/ValueInvestingStyle.html.

Sirri, E. R., & Tufano, P. (1998). Costly Search and Mutual Fund Flows. The Journal of Finance, 53(5), 1589-1622.

Spatt, C. S. (2005). Speech by SEC Staff: Conflicts of Interest in Asset Management. Hedge Fund Regulation and Compliance Conference. New York City.

Stier, C., Calvin, J., Krentzman, E., & Weisman, A. (2010). Fund Managers and the New Regulatory Reality: What Can You Expect?. Financial Foresight, 8(2).

Stockton, K., & Shtekhman, A. (2010). A Primer on Tactical Asset Allocation Strategy Evaluation. Valley Forge.

Swinkels, L. A. P. (2007). Have Pension Plans Changed after the Introduction of IFRS? Rotterdam.

Tartler, J. (2009). Berliner Gipfel - Wie die EU die Märkte anketten will. Financial Times Deutschland. Retrieved November 2010, from http://www.ftd.de/politik/international/:berliner-gipfel-wie-die-eu-die-maerkte-anketten-will/478067.html.

Tilmes, R. (2002). Financial Planning im Private Banking (3rd ed.). Bad Soden: Uhlenbruch Verlag.

Treynor, J. L. (1965). How to Rate Management of Investment Funds. Harvard Business Review, 43(1), 63-75.

Truman, E. M. (2007). Sovereign Wealth Funds: The Need for Transparency and Accountability. Peterson Institute for International Economics Policy Brief, 7(6).

Truman, E. M. (2008). A Blueprint for Sovereign Wealth Fund Best Practices. Peterson Institute for International Economics Policy Brief, 8(3), 1-21. Peterson Institute for International Economics.

U.S. Department of Labor (2010). Compliance Assistance. Retrieved December 20, 2010, from http://www.dol.gov/ebsa/compliance_assistance.html.

Urwin, R. (2008). Best Practice in Investment Governance for Pension Funds. Governance, an International Journal of Policy and Administration.

Vanderhei, J., & Holden, S. (2006). 401(k) Plan Asset Allocation, Account Balances, and Loan Activity in 2005. Washington.

Vanderhei, J., Holden, S., & Alonso, L. (2009). 401(k) Plan Asset Allocation, Account Balances, and Loan Activity in 2008. Washington.

Vanderhei, J., Holden, S., & Alonso, L. (2010). 401(k) Plan Asset Allocation, Account Balances, and Loan Activity in 2009. Washington.

Vanderhei, J., Holden, S., Alonso, L., & Copeland, C. (2009). 401(k) Plan Asset Allocation, Account Balances, and Loan Activity in 2007. Washington.

Vanderhei, J., Holden, S., Copeland, C., & Alonso, L. (2007). 401(k) Plan Asset Allocation, Account Balances, and Loan Activity in 2006. Washington.

Verordnung zur Durchführung des Gesetzes über das öffentliche Versorgungswesen (DVVersoG) (1994). Bayerisches Staatsministerium des Innern.

Verordnung über die Anlage des gebundenen Vermögens von Versicherungsunternehmen (Anlageverordnung - AnlV) (2010). Berlin: Deutscher Bundestag.

Verordnung über die Beaufsichtigung der Versicherungsunternehmen und der Versorgungswerke der Freien Berufe in Nordrhein-Westfalen (Versicherungsaufsichtsverordnung - VersAufsVO NRW) (2010). Finanzministerium Nordrhein-Westfalen im Benehmen mit der Bundesanstalt für Finanzdienstleistungen.

Verordnung über die Rechnungslegung von Versicherungsunternehmen (Versicherungsunternehmens-Rechnungslegungsverordnung - RechVersV) (2009). Berlin: Deutscher Bundestag.

Vittas, D. (1996). Pension Funds and Capital Markets. Public Policy for the Private Sector, 71.

Walter, I. (1998). The Global Asset Management Industry: Competitive Structure, Conduct and Performance. New York City.

Wehrle, L. S. (1961). Life Insurance Investment: The Experience of Four Companies. Yale Economic Essays, 1, 70–136.